The Revolutionary War Tourist

Visiting the Battlefields and Historic Sites of the American Revolution

By Lenny Flank

Red and Black Publishers, Florida

© copyright 2018 by Red and Black Publishers

Contents

Introduction 5
Jamestown 9
Boston Massacre 15
Boston Tea Party 23
Second Virginia Convention 31
Revere's (And Dawes' and Prescott's) Ride 37
Lexington and Concorde 43
Fort Ticonderoga 49
Bunker Hill 55
Quebec City 61
Moore's Creek 65
Fort Sullivan 71
Independence Hall 75
Long Island 81
Bushnell's Turtle 87
Harlem Heights 91
Valcour Island 95
White Plains 101
Fort Washington 105
Washington's Crossing 109
Princeton 115
Fort Ticonderoga Siege 119
Oriskany 125
Bennington 133
Brandywine 137
Saratoga 143
Paoli 149
Liberty Bell Shrine 153
Valley Forge 159

Monmouth 165
Wyoming Valley 171
Fort Boonesborough 175
Vincennes 181
The War At Sea 187
Savannah 195
Castillo San Marcos 201
Charleston 205
Camden 211
Kings Mountain 217
Mobile 223
Cowpens 227
Guilford Courthouse 233
Eutaw Springs 239
Yorktown 243
The American in the Tower of London 251
Cape Canaveral 255
Treaty of Paris 259

Introduction

The Colonial Revolution of 1775 to 1783 has over the centuries become the subject of mythologizing by Americans. As our national origin story, this legend has grown to encompass a political and social outlook that still influences us today. According to this myth, the whole of the American colonial population, burdened with high taxes imposed upon them by an autocratic monarchy headed by King George III, rose up against their oppressors to seek independence and, virtually single-handedly against tremendous odds, managed to beat the best troops that the British Empire could muster and win their fight for freedom and democracy.

The historical reality, however, is different. The colonists actually paid a much lower rate of taxes than people in England itself did. There was no absolute monarchy in London: George III was not much more than a figurehead, and the British Empire was run by a parliamentary government headed by a Prime Minister: the King's only influence was that which he could exercise upon the Cabinet members. (Unfortunately, however, King George *did* have influence over many of the Cabinet members, and his stubbornness did much to exacerbate the situation as the American conflict became a proxy fight for feuding British political factions.)

The American colonists, meanwhile, were themselves deeply divided, with never any more than one-third of the population supporting the rebels, and another one-third remaining Loyalist and supporting the British Government—giving the American Revolution the character of a civil war. The American General Horatio Gates had a brother-in-law serving as a British officer; even that most ardent of Patriots, Benjamin Franklin, had a son who was a devoted Loyalist. In many battles, units of local militia were serving on both sides, and neighbor was shooting at neighbor. With the hindsight of victory, we refer to those who supported the rebellion as "Patriots", but in fact both sides viewed themselves as patriotic and devoted, and viewed the other side as disloyal and treacherous. Other people, though, just wanted the fighting to stop, and many switched from one side to the other and back again, according to whomever was winning at the time.

The original goal of the revolution was not separation from England, but the right to elect their own colonial representatives within the British Parliamentary government. "Independence" did not become the political objective until the war was already over a year old.

The Continental Army under George Washington lost most of its battles, and would never have won the war at all if it had not been for the money and supplies sent by France and Spain—most importantly a contingent of French troops and a fleet from the French Navy. The British, on the other hand, never sent their best troops or generals to America and never really focused their full attention on the war there. They were too tied up with the global war against France and Spain, of which the

North American conflict was only a small and, to London, relatively unimportant part—Parliament was much more concerned with protecting the far richer and more important British colonies in the Caribbean and Asia.

The American rebellion was also very much a class-based affair: most of the Patriot leaders were the wealthy elite of colonial society, men who owned large businesses or plantations and who had substantial financial interests in the Revolution. They may have had lofty-sounding ideals, but they were also in it for the money. (On the other side, similarly, many Loyalist leaders were also wealthy traders and merchants who did not want to lose the commercial ties to England that had made them rich.)

And of course after the United States won independence, the lofty ideals of the Revolution took a decidedly anti-democratic bent: only white male property-owners were allowed to vote. Women were treated as little better than property—and African-Americans *were* legally property. The American struggle towards real democracy, with liberty and justice for all, was long, hard, and often bloody—and it is still not finished yet today.

In one of history's oddities, the United States, which had itself been born in a violent anti-colonial revolution, eventually went on to become the single most powerful force in the world supporting neo-colonialism and opposing anti-colonial rebellions all over the globe. During the Cold War, America was propping up dozens of unelected Third World military dictators who mercilessly slaughtered their own people—all in the name of "defending democracy".

And indeed, in many ways, the American Revolution paralleled another "war of national liberation" which the United States itself faced almost 200 years later: the Vietnam War. The roles, however, were now reversed: in the American Revolution, the British were the imperial world power and the Americans were the colonists struggling to become independent from foreign domination. In the Vietnam war, the Americans were the imperial world power and the Vietnamese were the colonials fighting for independence. (The Viet Minh rebels had even symbolically based their statement of independence on our own Declaration.)

In the end, however, the Viet Cong were able to defeat the Americans using the same methods that the Americans had once used to beat the British. Both the American colonists and the VC understood that their war was really political in nature, not military, and because of this both knew that they did not have to win on the battlefield—they only needed to not lose. Both used political actions to win the support of part of the population, then used terrorist organizations to intimidate the rest into acquiescence. Both depended upon powerful allies who gave them decisive material and political support. Both were hugely outclassed militarily, but were still able to use effective insurgent tactics to wear their enemy down in an endless low-level meat grinder that drained the imperial power of resources, and eventually became enormously unpopular back home and led to a political settlement.

Over the years, I have visited many of the battlefields and historical sites of the American Revolution. So this book is part travelogue, describing the history and places of interest in battlefield parks like Saratoga, Bunker Hill, Valley Forge, Lexington, and Cowpens—sites that are still an important part of our national mythology.

But it is also a historical study, presenting the history of the American Revolution as it actually was, peeling away the legend and looking at the reality. Because that reality, too, is still an important part of our national character today, and remains an essential ingredient in who we Americans are as a nation.

Jamestown

To understand the roots of the rebellion in the English colonies in 1775, we must understand the history, structure and economics of the colonial system that tied Great Britain to her North American possessions.

After Columbus reached the New World in 1492, the Spanish focused their attention on extracting gold and silver from South America, and most of North America was largely forgotten. It was the British who would in the end most successfully colonize North America.

By this time, the British monarchy was, essentially, no more. The King (or Queen) was still the titular head of state and, at least in theory, the British Government worked for the Crown, but in reality Parliament held all the actual power. Run by a Prime Minister, the parliamentary government made all the decisions—including the crucial and central task of setting the budget. Two political factions, the Tories and the Whigs, contested with each other for control.

The North American colonial venture was the work of the London Company, a joint stock corporation that had been formed under charter by King James I of England. The London Company's charter granted it rights to the southern half of the American coast, while the Plymouth Company was granted a charter for the northern half of the coast.

The first successful British settlement in North America was founded in Jamestown in 1607. This venture was run by a division of the London Company called the Virginia Company. Virginia Company shares sold in England for 12 pounds each. (William Shakespeare was a stockholder.)

While the Virginia Company was a for-profit venture hoping to find gold and other riches, it was also a social program utilized by the Crown Government to rid England of "excess population". In the move from agrarian feudalism towards a modern industrial economy, the English aristocracy had removed huge numbers of peasant serfs from the countryside by converting tracts of land from agrarian use into rental properties, and grew rich by leasing this land to the sheepherders who were needed to feed England's huge wool-cloth industry. The former serfs, now landless and moneyless, crowded into the urban areas. Some of these desperately poor people found employment as workers in England's growing factory system, but a large number still remained unemployed and hopeless, living in the streets as beggars, prostitutes and thieves. Various efforts to remove them—by imprisoning them for vagrancy, by impressing them into the Royal Navy, or by locking them up in poorhouses—all failed. The growing number of poor and landless led to political unrest in England; the Midlands Revolt and the rebellions of the Levelers and the Diggers were all based on the demands of dispossessed peasant serfs for land.

In 1609, the Virginia Company offered a way for the British Government to "ease the citie and suburbs of a swarme of unnecessarie inmates" by removing them all and sending them to the Company's new American colony in Jamestown, Virginia. In 1618, Parliament passed an act allowing the Virginia Company to round up the city's "vagabonds", with the Company promising to "sweepe your streets and washe your dores from idele persons, and the children of idele persons, and imploy them". People as young as eight years were now rounded up and shipped off to Virginia as "indentured servants" of the Company.

Reconstructed Fort at Jamestown

The Virginia Company painted a glowing portrait of its American colony to stockholders and potential colonists. America, they declared, was a land of plenty, which had "alle things in abundance, as in the firste creation, without toile or labour . . . In all the worlde a like abundance is not to be founde."

The Company, of course, knew better. The Jamestown colony was a death trap from the very beginning. The colonists, who had no idea how to survive in the

American wilderness, died at horrific rates. In the first winter alone, known as "The Starving Times", only 70 of the original 215 colonists survived. As large numbers of voluntary colonists and involuntary "vagabonds" began being shipped from England, the death toll rose steadily. In 1619, 165 children, age 8 to 16, arrived in Jamestown from the slums of London; by 1625, all but 12 were dead. One stockholder in London, poring over Company records, calculated that the Virginia Company had sent a total of 6000 people to Jamestown. Of these, only 1200 were still alive.

Archaeological excavation

Not all of these had died of starvation. The Company officials, particularly those who managed the colony's fabulously profitable tobacco and rice plantations, treated the colonists as virtual slaves. Abuse and beatings were routine, and forced over-work took its toll, particularly among the children—ninety percent of whom died within three years of arrival. Many colonists ran away to join the local Native American tribes; when found, they were hanged or beaten to death.

The desertion rate soon became so high that the Company was forced to make conciliatory measures. In 1619, the Company allowed a group of 22 representatives to be elected by the land-owning colonists—they formed a House of Burgesses that shared power with the Company-appointed Governor. America's first democratically elected representative assembly, therefore, was a desperate effort by a tyrannical Corporation to prevent its own people from fleeing.

In 1624, the British government, horrified by the stories it was hearing from the colonists, revoked the Virginia Company's charter and placed the colony under direct Parliamentary authority. The Royal Governor and the House of Burgesses became the Crown Government's intermediary, and by 1700 all the other English colonies in America had adopted similar elected Assemblies to exercise local self-rule. These were in turn overseen by a committee of Parliament in London known as the Lords of Trade.

A total of 13 British colonies were established by Royal Charter in American territory. Some of these were granted as sole proprietorships to a single owner (the Pennsylvania colony, for instance, was chartered as the personal property of William Penn). Others were founded by charters granted to joint stock companies (the Massachusetts Bay Company and the Virginia Company being examples). Like all Royal Charters, the colonies were tightly controlled by the British government. Under the mercantile system, colonies were viewed as simply ways of siphoning wealth from foreign territories and sending it back to the homeland. Many of the colonial charters spelled out how trade was to be conducted in the colonies, with England having special privileges (including, in some cases, the right that all colonial trade had to be with, or at least go through, England). A series of laws known as the Navigation Acts formalized these restrictions, limiting the amount of manufacturing that the colonists could do (forbidding them outright from making their own iron cooking pots, for example), and essentially turning the colonies into a source of raw materials for British industry and a captive market for the finished products.

In this commercial relationship was planted the seeds of the American Revolution.

Today, the Jamestown site is part of the Colonial National Historic Park near Williamsburg VA (which also contains the nearby Yorktown battlefield) and is run by the US National Park Service. In 1893, when the exact site of Fort James was unknown, a portion of Jamestown Island was donated to a private conservation group. The NPS obtained another 1500 acres on the island in 1934 and began archaeological excavations in the 1950s, which eventually discovered the original site of the Fort in 1996. Today that location is owned by Preservation Virginia, a statewide nonprofit group which protects historical sites, and the rest of the park is owned by the National Park Service. There is a walking trail that winds through the site, and displays of original building foundations including houses, a gunsmithery, a glassware factory, a tavern, and the home of Governor John Harvey.

Next door to the National Park is the Jamestown Settlement, a state-owned recreation of the colonial village with living history re-enactors. There is an exhibit hall with artifacts recovered from the site, and replicas of the three English ships—*Susan Constant, Godspeed*, and *Discovery*—which brought most of the original colonists to Virginia.

Boston Massacre

March 5, 1770

Massachusetts

By 1750, the continent of North America was divided between three European empires. The Spanish had control of what is now Mexico and the southwestern United States, which was known as "New Spain". The French claimed Quebec and the entire Mississippi River drainage in the center of the continent, which they called "New France". And in "New England", the British had established a series of colonies along the coast from Canada to Georgia. On the European continent, these three countries had been vying with each other for hundreds of years and had fought nearly constant wars amongst themselves. Now, the New World colonies were also a source of hostility between them.

This set the stage for yet another war between France and England, from 1756 to 1763. Known in Europe as the "Seven Years War", it would be the first truly global conflict, with battles fought over control of colonies and trade routes in Asia, Africa, and the New World. But the primary focus of the struggle was in North America, where an alliance of French Army forces and local Native American tribes faced off against the British Army and colonial militias. The North American theater became known as the "French and Indian War".

It was in the aftermath of this war that the seeds of rebelliousness were first planted. The English realized that they needed an alliance with the Native Americans in the west to help prevent French or Spanish expansion. So as a matter of policy, London banned the American colonists from any settlement west of the Appalachian Mountains: this area was intended to become a Native American homeland called "Indiana", which would serve as a bulwark against the other European powers. The colonists, however, coveted these fertile areas and openly defied the Crown Government by settling there anyway. It was a cause of friction.

With its unprecedented global scale, moreover, the Seven Years War was expensive to fight, and it severely depleted the British treasury. Since the war had been fought largely with the aim of defending the North American colonies from the French, the British Lords of Trade decided that at least some of the burden of paying for it should also fall upon them, and Parliament passed a number of new taxes to raise money specifically to pay for the defense and administration of the colonies. The Sugar Act of 1764 and the Stamp Act of 1765 produced little debate in Parliament, and passed quickly and routinely without any opposition.

In the colonies, however, these taxes provoked widespread resistance, to the utter and unexpected shock of the Crown government. In a series of respectful but assertive communications, the Americans objected to the imposition of any taxes as long as the colonial governments had no voice in Parliament, and asserted that only their own elected Assemblies and Houses of Burgesses had the legal authority to levy taxes in the colonies. In London, the Whig faction supported the colonials in their argument. After bitter political fighting in Parliament, the taxes were withdrawn.

In 1768, however, the British Government once again attempted to impose a series of taxes under the Townshend Revenue Act, which set an import duty on glass, paper, tea, and paint—all of which were products that were shipped solely from England. The money was intended to pay for colonial administration, but the colonists objected once again to "taxation without representation" and a boycott appeared against the taxed goods and quickly spread. The colonial Massachusetts House of Representatives sent a formal petition to King George III asking for the taxes to be repealed, and sent messages to the other colonial legislatures to join them in the protest. The unrest quickly spread, and this time, in October 1768, London responded by sending 4,000 British Army troops to Boston. Billeted in private homes throughout the city, these soldiers now made up about one-fifth of the entire population of Boston. Although there were no acts of resistance against the troops, the colonials deeply resented what they came to view as an occupying "foreign" army.

The breaking point came on March 5, 1770. That evening, an apprentice wigmaker named Garrick was walking past the Customs House (now the Old State House) when he saw a British Army officer entering and accused him of owing money to the wig shop. Hearing the commotion, the British soldier on sentry duty at the building, Private Hugh White, approached Garrick and demanded that he show respect to the officer. The two argued, and White hit the apprentice on the side of the head with the butt of his musket. This in turn attracted a crowd of onlookers who began to heckle White. Someone rang the local church bell (which served as the fire alarm), and this attracted an even larger crowd. Soon the small courtyard outside the Customs House was packed with at least sixty angry Bostonians.

Boston Massacre marker

White, fearing for his safety, retreated inside the building, and a message was sent to a nearby barracks asking for more troops. A group of eight soldiers led by Captain Thomas Preston arrived and formed a line in front of the building entrance. They carried loaded muskets and fixed bayonets, but, as everyone in town knew, they were under strict orders not to fire a weapon inside the city without an express command from a representative of the royal government. So the crowd, feeling emboldened, pelted the "redcoats" with snowballs and lumps of coal and mockingly ordered them to fire their guns, as Captain Prescott tried to impose order and disperse the mob, which now numbered several hundred.

Gravesite of Boston Massacre victims

Then, at about 9:30pm, someone threw a wooden club which struck Private Hugh Montgomery in the head, knocking him to the ground. Seconds later, one of the British troops leveled his musket and fired into the crowd, and over the next minute or so a series of shots rang out as Prescott, who had given no order to fire, tried to stop them. When it ended, three civilians lay dead on the cobblestones and ten more were wounded (two of these would die later).

The shootings caused a sensation in the local press, but also a mixed reaction. Rebel leader Sam Adams, in a series of speeches and articles, dubbed it the "Boston

Massacre", and a printed engraving was circulated by another rebel, Paul Revere, depicting the troopers intentionally leveling their muskets and firing a volley into the unarmed crowd. Some colonial newspapers, however, echoed by the Whigs in London, viewed the event as a calculated act on the part of the colonials to inflame passions and provoke needless bloodshed. The funeral of the shooting victims attracted a crowd of over 10,000 — most of the city's population.

The eight soldiers were arrested and charged with murder. They were defended in court by attorney John Adams, the cousin of revolutionary firebrand Sam Adams and himself an ardent supporter of colonial rights. John Adams not only viewed the Massacre as an unnecessary provocation, but also wanted to demonstrate the impartiality of the colonial courts. At trial, six of the British soldiers, including Captain Prescott, were acquitted, and two others were convicted of manslaughter and sentenced to minor punishment.

In London, the British government tried to prevent further conflict, and ordered that all of the Army troops be moved out of the city of Boston and encamped on Castle Island, away from the civilians. To further defuse the situation, the Royal Government agreed to rescind all of the taxes imposed by the Townshend Act except one — the import tax on tea.

Almost a century later, the Boston Massacre was adopted as a symbol by the anti-slavery abolitionist movement, since one of the people killed in the shooting was an African-American sailor named Crispus Attucks. In 1888 all five Massacre victims were relocated to the Granary Burying Ground near the Commons, where they were re-interred together.

Today, a stone circle in the courtyard of the Old State House commemorates the place where the Boston

Massacre took place. The spot is one of the stops on the Freedom Trail, a 2.5 mile walking path established in 1952, marked by brick patterns on the sidewalk, that connects 16 of the historic sites in Boston, including the Paul Revere House, Boston Commons, Faneuil Hall, and the Old State House. The National Park Service runs a visitors center at Boston Commons.

Boston Tea Party

December 16, 1773

Massachusetts

In colonial times, the single biggest trans-Atlantic trade item was tea, which was, after the unrest in 1770, still subject to tax. This was enough by itself to cause resentment among colonial merchants and traders, and an entire black-market economy appeared in the colonies, in which independent traders and smugglers would illegally import tax-free tea from the Dutch and sell it below the price of the British product. For some Americans, evading the British trade monopoly (and the tea tax) was a patriotic duty and a political protest: for others, it was simple greed. Many prominent Boston merchants—including several of the rebel leaders like John Hancock, one of the wealthiest men in the British colonies—grew rich through this illegal black market.

But Parliament then worsened the situation when the British East India Company, which owned all the tea production in India, found itself facing difficulties. In 1772, Europe went through an economic downturn, and tea sales plummeted. To get out of this difficulty, the Company decided to sell its surplus stocks of tea to the American colonists at a sharply reduced price, beating the Dutch smugglers in the market and recapturing their monopoly. To aid the ailing company (and to re-assert its right to tax the colonials), in May 1773 the British Government agreed to suspend the collection of the royal tax on the Company's exported tea from England—but to continue collecting the tax that the colonists paid on this same tea when it was sold in America. Further, the tea would be sold only through selected outlets in America, known as "tea agents", which the Company would control. The East India Company would have sole legal monopoly over the tea trade.

The American colonists (especially the tea smugglers) exploded in protest. Newspapers thundered against the tea tax and the monopoly, and boycotts were called. Contrary to what many believe today, the colonists were not protesting against unreasonably high tax rates: the tea tax was a mere pittance, just a few pennies per pound, and brought barely 300 pounds sterling into the English treasury each year. Indeed, the price of the British tea was actually far *lower* now under the new laws than it had been before: after independence, the United States government would itself place a tax on tea that was higher than the one imposed now by the British. It was not the tax itself that the colonials were opposed to, though, but the fact that they had not consented to it or approved it, and they had no elected representatives in Parliament to do so.

In the larger sense, however, the political conflict was just the symptom of a deeper cultural clash. At first, the colonials had always been offended by the label "American": as the descendents of white Europeans, they considered themselves fully "British", and not like those other English colonies in "uncivilized" Africa and Asia.

Over time, however, isolated on the other side of the ocean with their own governmental institutions, the colonials had indeed developed their own distinctive "American" culture in which many of the elements of traditional English custom had fallen away. The heavy aristocratic class that dominated English society did not exist in the colonies, who, although they had sharp economic distinctions of their own, viewed themselves as more socially egalitarian. The conservative Church of England held little sway in America: instead, religious dissent was rife and the freedom of conscience was cherished. And the colonial political institutions—the Assemblies and the Houses of Burgesses—were, though severely restricted in power, much freer and more democratic than the British Parliamentary structure. Although they still considered themselves as British citizens, when the colonial rebels now referred to themselves as "Patriots", it was loyalty to "America" which they were claiming. The divide between "America" and "England" had already begun to deepen.

Pamphlets quickly appeared in the streets warning that any company tea agent who accepted the taxed tea would receive a visit from rebel "Sons of Liberty" bullyboys. This was an underground organization, recruited by Sam Adams and dating back to the time of the Stamp Act, of what were in effect political terrorists. They had a habit of intimidating and sometimes beating up (or of "tarring and feathering") opponents and/or burning down their house, and often used threats to ensure conformity to the declared boycott. This approach was made necessary because the Patriots never had the active support of a majority of the colonial population.

The threats worked: by the winter of 1773 all the appointed agents in New York, Philadelphia, and Charleston had resigned, and, with no one to receive them, British cargo ships which arrived in the harbor carrying tea from England were turned away, as the colonial governors decided to avoid a potential conflict.

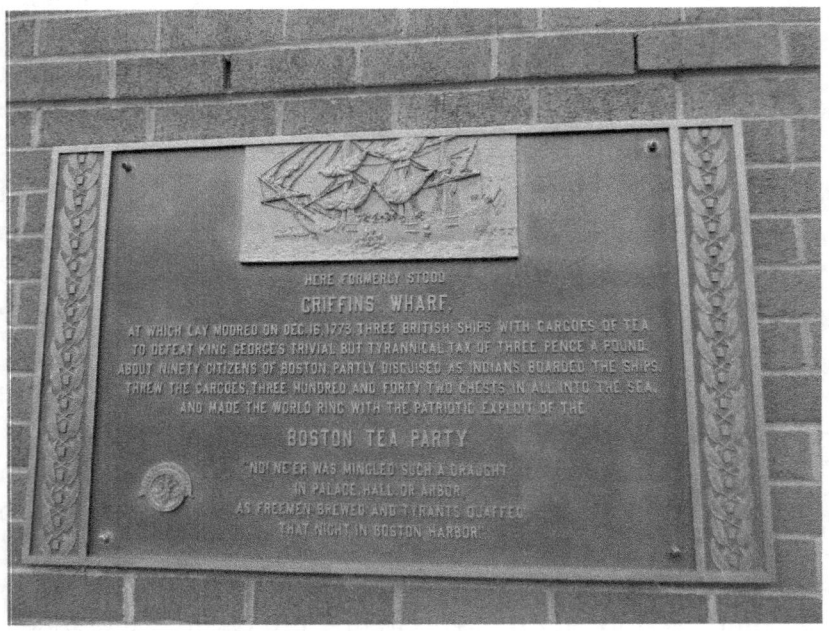

Historical marker at the site of the Boston Tea Party

In Boston, however, Royal Governor Thomas Hutchinson decided to make a stand and demonstrate his authority. On November 28, the cargo ship *Dartmouth* arrived from England with 114 chests of tea and anchored at Griffin Wharf. Hutchinson announced that the tea would be unloaded and the tax collected and paid. But at a town meeting held in nearby Faneuil Hall, Boston residents, urged on by Sam Adams and the rebels, resolved that the tax would not be paid and demanded that the ship instead return to London. A group of 25 men was appointed to surround the wharf and prevent the cargo from being unloaded. On December 15, two more tea ships, the *Beaver* and the *Eleanor*, arrived and docked next to the *Dartmouth*: they too were placed under watch.

Governor Hutchinson, meanwhile, was powerless to do anything—all of the British troops remained confined to Castle Island under crown order, where they had been isolated after the Boston Massacre. The streets of Boston belonged to the rebels.

But the insurgents were facing a deadline. Under British regulations, if the tax had not been paid by December 17 the royal customs house would be able to confiscate the cargo and collect the tax from their sale. So, on the night of December 16, at another town meeting, the rebels decided that they would take steps of their own to prevent the tea from being sold. Under the direction of Sam Adams, a group of 60-70 Sons of Liberty, some of them thinly disguised as Mohawk warriors, made their way to Griffin Wharf, swarmed aboard all three ships, and dumped 40-some tons of tea into Boston Harbor. History would come to know it as the "Boston Tea Party".

Boston Tea Party replica ships and museum

The effects of this protest were drastic for both sides. In England, the Whigs, who had given political support to the colonies and their grievances, now viewed the "Destruction Of The Tea" as a lawless act of vandalism and a violation of the rights of private property, and many of them turned against the American rebels. The British Crown Government condemned the colonials as a "tumultuous and noisy rabble" and "brigands", immediately demanded that the city government pay the East India Company for the lost tea (worth about $2 million in today's money), and closed the Port of Boston to all commercial shipping until this was done. In a series of resolutions that became known in America as the "Intolerable Acts", Parliament declared that the colony of Massachusetts was in "open rebellion", suspended the colonial government, declared martial law in Boston, released the soldiers from Castle Island, and forced Boston's civilians to provide billets for the troops. Boston once again became an occupied city. The other American colonies, watching from afar, realized that they might be next. It strengthened the rebel movement across the entire continent.

The protesters, meanwhile, now concluded that conflict with London was inevitable, and began preparing. Across the colonies, rebel groups formed "Committees of Correspondence" to organize resistance and to communicate news and information. Local militias began to stockpile muskets, cannons and gunpowder—it was said that they could be ready to fight on a minute's notice, earning them the nickname "Minutemen". In Boston, an extensive intelligence network was formed to keep an eye on British troop movements. Both sides had now chosen a path that would inexorably lead to revolution and war.

Today, the exact location of the old Griffin's Wharf, where the Tea Party took place, is a matter of some controversy, but a historical plaque marks the spot where most scholars have concluded the Wharf once stood. The Boston Tea Party and Ships Museum is also located here, with a display of exhibits and artifacts (including one of the original tea crates) and replicas of two of the cargo ships that were boarded by the rebels that night.

Second Virginia Convention

March 23, 1775

Richmond VA

In the wake of the "Intolerable Acts", Sam Adams wrote a letter circulated through the Committees of Correspondence to the other colonies, pointing out that Massachusetts was fighting for the rights as Englishmen of all American colonials, and that the repressive actions unleashed on Boston could well fall upon them in the future. A convention in Massachusetts issued the "Suffolk Resolves", declaring that any King who trampled the rights of his subjects in this manner no longer deserved their allegiance. As a result, a wave of support for the rebels spread up and down the American coast. With Boston Harbor closed and the colony's trade cut off, sympathetic merchants and farmers from Georgia to New York flooded the city with food, clothing and money. A boycott of English trade goods was called by the Committees of Correspondence, and expressions of support came from most of the colonial Assemblies.

By the middle of 1774, most of the more radical Committee leaders decided that it was necessary to form a united movement. In September, rebel delegates from all 13 colonies met in the "First Continental Congress" to formulate a common list of demands, coordinate their response to actions of the Royal Government, and attempt to usurp the political initiative from the royal colonial governors. One of their first acts was to adopt the Suffolk Resolves, pledging that if Boston were subjected to military attack, the other colonies would come to her aid—but urging that Massachusetts show restraint and not provoke the conflict. The Congress also issued, in a petition addressed to the King, a list of rights to which they were entitled as Englishmen, at the top of which was the "free and exclusive power of legislation in their provincial legislatures". While the demands of the Continental Congress once again found political support among some of the Whig faction in London, the Parliament, with the active encouragement of King George, took a harsh stand against it.

Most colonial eyes now turned to Virginia. The largest and richest of the 13 colonies, Virginia's actions would settle the matter for many of the other colonies as well. When word reached Virginia of the events in Boston, delegates from the House of Burgesses assembled in the capitol at Williamsburg in 1774 and declared their support for the Boston rebels. This brought immediate reaction from Royal Governor John Dunmore, who had held the office since 1771. He dissolved the Burgesses and forbade it from meeting again. In response, the delegates gathered a short time later in the Burgesses Chamber at Williamsburg (while Dunmore was away with the militia) and declared themselves the "Virginia Convention". They again announced their support for the rebellion, elected delegates to the Continental Congress, and endorsed a boycott of British tea.

When it became apparent that Parliament was not going to give in to the colonial demands and there would be no political solution, a Second Virginia Convention was called in March 1775. This meeting took place in the St John's Episcopal Church in Richmond, which was far enough away from the capitol at Williamsburg that the delegates could make a getaway if Governor Dunmore sent troops to arrest them.

Patrick Henry gives his speech

The Convention debated its options for a few days until one of the delegates, a local lawyer named Patrick Henry, introduced three proposals calling for the formation of a local militia which would be under the command of a committee formed from the disbanded Burgesses. Each county in the state was to organize one company of militia from its local residents.

In effect, Henry's resolution was a declaration of war against the colony's Royal Government—it placed the elected Burgesses in political control and authorized armed force to protect it. Fierce debate followed. Some of the delegates were not yet willing to go that far, and still hoped for a peaceful political settlement. On March 23, Henry took the floor and gave a speech defending his resolution that secured his immortal place in American history. He declared that there was no hope of a peaceful solution, that war with England was inevitable, and that the colonies should begin preparing for it. Picking up an ivory letter opener and dramatically plunging it to his breast, he concluded, "I know not what course others may take, but as for me—give me liberty, or give me death!"

With Henry's impassioned defense, the resolutions passed by a small majority, and a call went out for militia volunteers. Within three weeks, the war foreseen by Henry had begun. After the Declaration of Independence in 1776, he became the Governor of the colonial government.

While Patrick Henry's "give me liberty or give me death" speech is one of the most famous ever given, it was not transcribed at the time and was not included in the written proceedings of the convention, so we have no contemporary record of exactly what he said. The version that is printed in the history books comes from a biography written in 1817 by a man named Wirt, almost 20 years after Henry had died. Wirt's account, in turn, is based almost entirely on a letter from Judge George Tucker, who had been present in St John's Church and who wrote it down for Wirt as best he could remember it. Tucker's original letter, sadly, has now been lost. Tucker was, however, said to have remarked later that he recalled Henry using some very rough language invoking the fear of a slave rebellion or incursions by Native Americans from the Ohio Valley to justify the formation of a militia, and that this was edited out by Wirt. So we can no longer be sure how much of "Patrick Henry's speech", including its stirring ending, actually came from him, how much came from Tucker, and how much came from Wirt.

Today, the St John's Episcopal Church in Richmond still functions as an active congregation and still holds worship services every Sunday. On other days, the local historical society gives guided tours of the building to interpret the Second Virginia Convention, Patrick Henry's speech, and their effect upon the American Revolution.

Revere's (And Dawes' and Prescott's) Ride

April 1775

Boston

After the Boston Tea Party and the occupation of Boston by English troops, all seemed calm. But under the surface, things had already reached the boiling point. The colonials had formed their own unofficial government—the Continental Congress—and it had resolved to use force to oppose any future British moves. Over the next few years, the insurgents also systematically took control of the local governments in all thirteen colonies, through the elected Assemblies and Houses of Burgesses. In effect, the real control of local political power on the ground had already shifted from faraway England to the colonies. In this sense, the Revolution had already been accomplished. The colonial rebels were in charge.

In the myriad of small towns around Boston, meanwhile, local militia "Minutemen", many of them veterans of the French and Indian War, were openly drilling in military maneuvers, and had built up stockpiles of gunpowder and cannons—all in preparation to face the British Army. The English commander in Boston, General Thomas Gage, of course knew all of this was going on, but delayed taking any actions against it. As a practical matter, he did not want to resort to bloodshed, and hoped that if he did not provoke any further reaction the rebellion would play itself out and an amicable political solution would be reached.

But in the spring of 1775 the Royal Government in London decided that it was time to act, and sent orders to Gage instructing him to confiscate the weapons that were being gathered by the rebels. Whether Parliament realized the implications of their decision or not, they had elected to start a war.

On April 18, Gage mustered a group of 700 redcoats from the 19th Regiment of Foot, under the command of Lieutenant-Colonel Francis Smith, and ordered them to march the 18 miles to Concord, where it was known that the colonials had stockpiled gunpowder, muskets and cannons. The British troops left just after dark, crossing the Charles River by boat and moving through Charlestown and up the Lexington Road, planning to march all night and reach Concord at dawn.

The colonials, meanwhile, had already organized an extensive spy network within Boston, under the direction of Dr Joseph Warren. By some accounts, Warren's sources extended right into General Gage's own house— to Gage's American-born wife. So Warren was already expecting that the British would undertake some sort of action, and when Smith's troops were ordered out, the American spymaster knew about it almost immediately.

By messenger, Warren summoned two members of the Boston rebel network—Paul Revere and William Dawes—to his house. Dawes was a leather tanner and a member of the Minutemen; Revere was a silversmith who had participated in the Boston Tea Party and who knew most of the rebel leaders in the Boston area. Each had already served before as couriers for the rebel spy network, and now both were given a horse and assigned the task of riding to Concord to alert the militia that the British Regulars were on their way. To increase their chances of getting the message through, each rider would travel along a different route: Revere would take a boat across the Charles River and then ride to Concord, while Dawes would take the longer land route across the Boston Neck. Using a pre-arranged signal, Revere would also alert the Charlestown militia by placing two lamps in the steeple of the Old North Church (the tallest structure in the area), indicating that the British redcoats were crossing the Charles River.

Old North Church

Warren's intelligence information also told him that the redcoats were going to stop in Lexington to arrest rebel leaders Sam Adams and John Hancock, who were both staying at a friend's house there. This information was actually incorrect, but, not knowing this, Revere met with the two leaders in Lexington just after midnight to warn them; Dawes arrived about half an hour later.

After a brief rest, the two then continued on towards Concord. Along the way they met up with another member of the courier network named Dr Samuel Prescott. By some accounts, he just happened to be riding along the road on his way home; more likely, Revere had arranged for Prescott to meet them there because he knew the area well and could act as a guide. The three set off together for Concord.

They didn't make it. Around 1:30 in the morning, the trio unexpectedly encountered a British patrol: this was part of a force of 200 redcoats under Major John Pitcairn who were marching ahead of Smith's column as an advance guard, with orders to protect the bridges along the road. The rebel couriers scattered. Dawes got away, but fell off his horse and ended up walking all the way back to Boston. Revere galloped into a small patch of woods, but was surrounded there and captured by the British. Only Prescott made it all the way to Concord, where he informed the local militia that the redcoats were on their way. The colonials quickly hid their supply of weapons and powder so the British wouldn't find it.

In Lexington, militia commander Captain John Parker gathered up his Minutemen and assembled them on the Lexington Commons to await the redcoats. He hoped to stop the British, or at least delay them long enough to allow the weapons in Concord to be moved out of danger.

Revere, meanwhile, was taken along by the British as a prisoner. But as they approached Lexington, the redcoats could hear the alarm shots being fired in front of them by Minutemen sentries and lookouts and realized that there might be a confrontation, and, not wanting to be bogged down with a prisoner and not knowing what else to do with him, Pitcairn confiscated Revere's horse and let him go. He walked back to Lexington.

The site of Revere's capture

In 1860, American poet Henry Wadsworth Longfellow composed a long poem to commemorate the call to arms on that night. But Longfellow got the history all wrong. The "one if by land, two if by sea" signal in the church tower was mistakenly described as a signal to Revere, when in fact it was a signal *from* Revere to the Charlestown militia. Dawes and Prescott were dropped entirely from the account, Revere's capture wasn't mentioned, and he was wrongly depicted as the lone rider who dashed all the way to Concord and heroically turned out the militia. Nevertheless, it is Longfellow's inaccurate version that is known by every American schoolchild, while the actual history of Prescott, Dawes and Revere has largely faded from memory.

Two other subsequent riders, also members of the colonial communications network, have also disappeared from history. After the clashes at Lexington and Concord, the rebel courier system was activated again to spread the word that the long-expected war had begun. The first of these was Israel Bissell, who rode all the way from Boston to Philadelphia, informing militia commanders and local newspapers along the way of the battles. Another rider was Sybil Ludington, a 16-year old girl, who rode from Boston to Connecticut to spread the news.

Today, Paul Revere's house is a part of the Freedom Trail in Boston, as is the Old North Church and the gravesite of William Dawes. At the Minuteman National Historical Park, just outside Lexington, is a monument marking the spot where Revere was captured by the British during his midnight ride.

Lexington and Concord

April 19, 1775

Massachusetts

The advance force of 200 British redcoats under Major John Pitcairn, after marching most of the night, reached Lexington at dawn on April 19, 1775. Although their orders had been to proceed as quickly as possible to Concord and to hold the bridge there, as they approached Lexington Major Pitcairn could see a group of around 75 colonial militiamen assembled on the town Commons, with weapons, and, on his own initiative, decided to stop and disarm them.

They were the local Minutemen militia commanded by Capt. John Parker, who had already been informed by Paul Revere and William Dawes that the British troops were approaching. As the sun was coming up, Parker assembled his militiamen in formation and gave them instructions to hold their ground but not to fire unless they were first fired upon. "But," he added, "if they mean to have a war, then let it begin here."

Pitcairn drew up his redcoats in front of the assembled militia, and ordered, "Throw down your arms! You villains, you rebels!" For several tense seconds, there was a standoff, with both lines of armed men warily eyeing each other. Then Parker made his decision—he ordered his militia to retreat and disperse. Men began drifting away in ones and twos, and it seemed as if the situation had been defused.

Then a single musket shot rang out.

The marker at Lexington Commons

Nobody knows who fired it, or from which line it came. Neither Parker nor Pitcairn had given any order to fire. It would later be famously referred to as "the shot heard round the world".

Immediately, a ragged volley of musketry was exchanged between both sides, as both officers tried to stop it. When order was restored and the smoke cleared, one British soldier had been wounded and Pitcairn's horse had been shot out from under him, while seventeen American militiamen lay on the ground—eight of them dead. The American Revolutionary War had begun.

Hurriedly, the militia retreated behind some nearby stone walls and into buildings, but there was no more shooting. By now, the main British force under Lt Col Francis Smith had reached Lexington, and together the two groups formed into marching order and continued on towards Concord, which was still several hours away. As they marched, the British could hear alarm shots and church bells ringing which traced their progress; meanwhile, the colonials sent messengers to all the nearby towns to rally the local militia. Although there were no further shots fired at the redcoats, they knew they were marching into a war zone.

The North Bridge at Concord

Once the British reached Concord, Smith divided his force into several groups. One detachment was assigned to guard the North Bridge; others fanned out in search of the colonial muskets and cannons that were known to be there. But Smith was too late. Most of the weaponry and gunpowder had already been removed by the insurgents and hidden elsewhere. Smith found only a small supply of gunpowder and some flour, which he burned.

Meanwhile, the Concord militia had assembled and marched towards the bridge, which was being held by the redcoats. As the colonials advanced into range, the British leveled their muskets and fired a volley. The Americans answered with a volley of their own, and after some more gunfire both sides withdrew.

After a fruitless four-hour search for the hidden weapons, Smith ordered his troops to form in column and began the 18-mile march back to Boston. But by this time, some 3,000 colonial militiamen had already made their way to Concord from the surrounding towns, and now they lay in wait along the road, hidden behind trees and boulders. For the rest of the afternoon, as the redcoats wearily marched along, the militiamen took constant potshots at them, then melted away whenever a group of British tried to pursue them. In Lexington, Smith once again ran into Parker's militia who had participated in the earlier exchange of gunfire and were now looking for revenge.

One bend in the road offered a particularly good ambush spot: it became known as "The Bloody Angle". The constant rain of musket balls from the woods did not stop even when Smith was joined by 1500 reinforcements sent from Boston under Lord Percy. By the time the redcoats reached Boston later that evening, they had suffered 73 troops killed and 174 wounded.

Gravesite of British troopers killed on the road from Concord

The British officials in Boston now realized that the colonial rebels were much better organized than they had thought, and that the Crown Government now faced the possibility of a real war. Lord Percy wrote to London, "Whoever looks upon them as an irregular mob will be much mistaken."

In response, Parliament relieved General Thomas Gage of command and sent three Army Generals—William Howe, John Burgoyne and Henry Clinton—to replace him. They were accompanied by several regiments of British Regulars and several thousand Hanover troops from Germany, allied with King George III. (Although only a portion of the Germans were from the principality of Hesse, the Americans took to referring to them all as "Hessians" and greatly resented the presence of what they considered to be "mercenaries".)

The three Generals thought that they would make quick work of these colonial rebels. (Burgoyne, it was said, had made a gentleman's bet with a friend that he would be back in London within a year after having routed the Americans.) They had no way of knowing what was in store for each of them.

Today, the Lexington and Concord battle sites are contained in two separate historical parks. The Lexington Commons, where the first shots were fired, is a State Park and a National Historic Landmark. It contains a number of stone markers, statues, and monuments, including the gravesite of several colonials killed in the battle.

The North Bridge at Concord, along with the various historical sites along the Lexington Road, is now part of the federal Minuteman National Historical Park, run by the National Park Service. The Minuteman Park consists of a 5 mile strip running along the historic road between Boston, Lexington and Concord, protecting about 970 acres. The site contains a driving tour, several miles of walking trails, and interpretive signs and displays, and covers sites including the North Bridge in Concord, the Bloody Angle, the Hartwell Tavern, and Fiske Hill. The NPS runs two Visitors Centers, one at North Bridge and the other along Battle Road.

The park also contains The Wayside, an 18th century home that was inhabited at various times by American writers Louisa May Alcott, Nathaniel Hawthorne, and Margaret Sidney. Just a few miles from the park is Walden Pond, made famous by American writer Henry David Thoreau.

Fort Ticonderoga

May 10, 1775

New York

With the combat at Lexington and Concord, the Continental Congress, which had till then been leading a political rebellion, now found itself in charge of thirteen fractious and contentious colonies that were suddenly at war with a global superpower. As one of its first acts, the Congress grandly announced the formation of a "Continental Army" under the command of a Virginia militia officer, "General" George Washington. It was an army that existed mostly on paper, however; the only troops it had were those which the colonial militias would agree to give it, and it had virtually no weapons, gunpowder, uniforms, tents, food, or other supplies.

But the colonials knew of at least one place where they could get it....

In 1755, the French had been making moves towards the British colonies in North America, sparking off the "French and Indian War". As part of their defenses, the

French built a large stone fort on the western shore of Lake Champlain, called Fort Carillon. This was a very strategic place: Lake Champlain, long and narrow, stretched all the way from the Canadian border to the Hudson River. Whoever controlled the Lake controlled the northern approaches to New York and Boston—and whoever controlled the Fort controlled the Lake. So in 1759 the British General Sir Jeffrey Amherst captured Fort Carillon and renamed it Fort Ticonderoga.

Fort Ticonderoga

After the French and Indian War, with the entire eastern seaboard firmly in British control, the Fort lost its strategic value, and was manned by a small outpost who only partially repaired its walls. But after the battles of Lexington and Concord, Fort Ticonderoga became of crucial importance to the Continental Army: fearing that British forces could move down from Canada to attack the colonial strongholds in Boston and Philadelphia, the Continental Congress decided to pre-empt this by invading Canada and defeating the British troops there. And Fort Ticonderoga was central to this plan: not only did it contain large supplies of muskets, gunpowder and cannons which were badly needed by the Continental Army, but the Fort lay directly along the pathway for the planned invasion.

So, just weeks after the war with Britain began, the Americans made plans to seize Fort Ticonderoga, which, they knew, was held by a tiny garrison of just 42 men. To take the Fort, the Congress turned to a Massachusetts militia commander named Benedict Arnold, who was now given the rank of Colonel in the Continental Army and 400 troops.

But when Arnold and his Continental soldiers marched from Massachusetts into Vermont and the eastern shore of Lake Champlain, they ran into a problem. A group of 200 local militia in Vermont, called the Green Mountain Boys, had also decided to organize an attack on Fort Ticonderoga. While the two forces agreed to work together to assault the Fort, a bitter argument broke out over who was in command: Benedict Arnold arguing that he held authority from the Continental Congress, and the Green Mountain Boys flatly refusing to follow anyone other than their elected "Colonel", Ethan Allen.

Eventually, a "joint command" agreement was reached which made everyone happy, and the two forces gathered on the shore of Lake Champlain, across from Fort Ticonderoga, at around 2 am on May 10, 1775. But now they ran into another problem: there were only two small ferryboats available—not big enough to carry all 600 soldiers. Running the boats back and forth across the Lake all night would attract the attention of the British defenders, and so after only two trips it was decided that the attack would be made at dawn with just the small force of Arnold's Regulars and Allen's militia, about 160 men, which had already crossed.

The approach to Fort Ticonderoga across Lake Champlain

Fort Ticonderoga was surrounded by massive stone walls and a heavy iron gate, but when the Americans got there, they found just one British soldier on guard duty. Swarming into the gateway, the colonials took the entire garrison by surprise: the British commander was rousted out of bed in his pajamas. Ethan Allen ceremoniously claimed possession of the fort "in the name of the great Jehovah and the Continental Congress". Not a single shot had been fired.

Arnold's army (and Allen's Green Mountain Boys) immediately began preparing for an invasion of Canada, using Fort Ticonderoga as their base. Once again, though, there was conflict between the two, as the Vermonters happily looted the British commander's supply of liquor. When Arnold tried to restore military discipline, the Green Mountain Boys simply refused to accept his authority: several times weapons were threateningly drawn on both sides.

Meanwhile, the Fort's 60 tons of supplies were distributed to the Continental Army, and its 59 cannons were dismantled and carried all the way to Boston for use in Washington's siege there, eventually forcing the British commander to withdraw from the city.

The capture of Fort Ticonderoga had an immediate effect on the morale of the Patriot rebels. With little in the way of popular support and with virtually no ability to wage large-scale warfare, the revolutionaries knew that their odds of success were slim. But the British surrender at Lake Champlain convinced them that perhaps they had a realistic chance after all.

The fall of Ticonderoga also had an unexpected effect on the British. With the lines of communication between Canada and New York now cut, the Crown Government was forced to set up two independent military commands in the north and south—there would be no single British commander-in-chief in North America. This lack of a unified strategic authority would have dire consequences for London throughout the entire war.

Today, Fort Ticonderoga is a National Historic Landmark near Plattsburg NY, on the shore of Lake Champlain. Following the War, the Fort was abandoned, donated to the state of New York in 1785, used to establish a small college for some time, then was sold to a private owner in 1820. By then, many of the walls had collapsed and the stones taken by nearby residents for use as building material. In 1908, the crumbled walls were restored and the site was opened to the public. In

1931 the land was donated to the Fort Ticonderoga Association, a nonprofit preservation group which has run the Fort as a museum since then. In 1960 Fort Ticonderoga was designated a Historic Landmark. There is a display of weaponry and artifacts, and living history presentations by re-enactors, including musket demonstrations and live cannon firings.

Bunker Hill

June 17, 1775

Massachusetts

It may be the most famous battle of the Revolutionary War. But the Battle of Bunker Hill did not happen the way most Americans today think it did. It didn't even happen on Bunker Hill. And it was the British who won the fight.

When the American Revolution began with the battles at Lexington and Concord, the bulk of the British Army was garrisoned in the city of Boston. The English government, hoping to quell the rebellion quickly, dispatched Generals Henry Clinton, John Burgoyne, and William Howe to Boston. They arrived in early June 1775.

While Boston was surrounded by towns filled with rebellious militia, the city itself was controlled by the British Navy. The only potential danger lay in the possibility that the colonial rebels might get cannons into position on some of the hills surrounding Boston, allowing them to shell the British ships in the harbor. To prevent that from happening, the British made plans to send troops to occupy the hills.

Through sympathetic civilians, the colonial militia commanders heard about the plan. To counter it, the rebel commander General Israel Putnam ordered Colonel William Prescott to take a force of about 1,000 Massachusetts and Connecticut militiamen and fortify Bunker Hill, which overlooked the harbor. Somehow, though, the colonial force ended up instead on Breed's Hill, about 600 yards away–perhaps because Prescott thought it would be easier to defend, perhaps because in the dark they simply went to the wrong hill. In any case, the colonials spent the night of June 16 digging trenches and building dirt and log breastworks on the crest of Breed's Hill. At daybreak, the British ship HMS *Lively* saw the fortifications and opened fire on them; within an hour most of the other warships in the harbor had joined in the bombardment. But by this time the Americans had already finished their redoubt, and the cannonade had little effect.

It fell to the British General Howe to remove the rebels. He went ashore with 2,500 troops at about 3pm on June 17. The Americans had about 1,000 militiamen on Breed's Hill; there were several hundred more on nearby Bunker Hill, but most of them refused to advance after seeing the British troops landing and moving towards the colonial position.

Howe probably thought his task would be easy. The American militia were, he believed, an undisciplined rabble, and his English regulars were the best army in the world–and they outnumbered the militiamen almost three to one. With a direct assault up the hill, Howe concluded, the colonials would break and run away, and the rebellion would be over. With supreme overconfidence, he formed his troops into an extended line, and ordered them to charge.

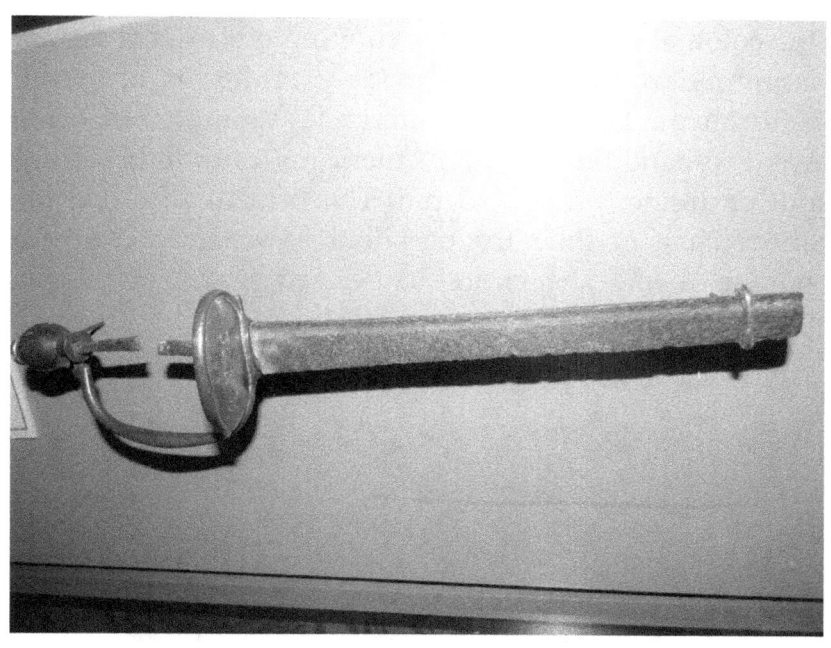

British officer's sword from Bunker Hill battlefield

In their redoubt, the Americans waited and watched as the red-coated British slowly came up the hill. According to legend, Colonel Prescott had issued the order, "Don't shoot until you can see the whites of their eyes." The British troops were only 30 yards away when the colonials opened fire. The effect was devastating: huge holes were ripped in the British ranks, and the entire line faltered, then staggered back down the hill. Dead redcoats lay everywhere. Howe hastily reorganized his troops, formed them into another line–and sent them back up the hill. Again the colonials opened fire at short range, and again the British dropped by the dozens and retreated. Howe was shocked; he had not expected an actual fight with the rebels.

He now ordered his artillery into action, and for some time, British cannon raked the Americans with canisters of grapeshot. And then, for the third time, the British troops were sent up Breed's Hill. By this time, however, the colonial militiamen were running out of powder and ammunition. The redcoats made it to the top of the hill with bayonets fixed, and after a few minutes of brutal hand-to-hand fighting, the Americans, outnumbered and out of ammo, broke and ran. The British, who had lost almost half of their troops killed or wounded, did not pursue them. The entire battle had lasted about two hours.

Bunker Hill monument

It was, technically, a British victory; the redcoats had driven their enemy off the battlefield and they stood in possession of the high ground. But it had been purchased at an unacceptably high cost, and the Americans had demonstrated an unexpected willingness to not only stand and fight, but to do so effectively. There would be no quick win here; the American insurgency would become a long bloody quagmire for the British.

Less than a year later, the American General Washington, using British cannons that had been captured from Fort Ticonderoga, once again occupied a series of hills around Boston. The British General Howe, surrounded by hostile civilians and cannons, abandoned the city, and withdrew his command post all the way to Canada.

In 1823, the Bunker Hill Monument Association, a local nonprofit citizens group, was formed to raise money to build a memorial at the site, and began construction of a 220-foot stone obelisk on the top of the hill. Financial difficulties twice brought a temporary halt to the project, and in the end it was completed only by selling most of the planned park property as housing lots. The obelisk was finally completed in 1842. In 1919, the Association turned the site over to the Massachusetts state government; it was then transferred to the National Park Service in 1976.

Today, Bunker Hill is a National Historical Park and part of the Boston "Freedom Trail" walking tour. In 2007, the Bunker Hill site underwent a restoration which repaired the obelisk, installed new lighting, and added better sidewalk and ramp access. A new museum was also added across the street from the obelisk, which displays a cyclorama painting of the battle and some artifacts recovered from the site.

Quebec City
December 31, 1775

Canada

With the capture of Fort Ticonderoga, the colonials were in a position to make a thrust into Canada, cutting off any British attempt to send troops down into New York. Washington planned a two-pronged attack. One American column of 1700 militia, led by General Philip Schuyler, would move north along Lake Champlain and capture Montreal. Another force of 1000, made up of two companies of Pennsylvania militia and Captain Daniel Morgan's riflemen from Virginia, all commanded by Colonel Benedict Arnold, would advance through Maine and take Quebec City.

At first, the invasion went smoothly. Although General Schuyler became sick and was replaced as commander by General Richard Montgomery, his troops reached Fort Jean outside Montreal on September 19 and began a siege. During some skirmishing, Ethan Allen and a group of Green Mountain Boys militia were captured by the British. The Canadian commander, General Guy Carleton, sent a small force of 900 men to try to lift the siege, but when it was repulsed, Fort Jean surrendered on November 3. Montreal was now defenseless, and surrendered without a shot on November 13.

Arnold's expedition did not go as well. The invasion plan depended upon the successful coordination and careful timing of two widely separated armies that had little communication with each other, and this was virtually impossible. The maps that Arnold had of Maine and Canada were, moreover, inaccurate and he underestimated the distance he would have to march in the freezing snow, leading him to run out of supplies. Many of his militia troops deserted or died.

When Arnold finally reached Quebec City on November 14, he dramatically demanded the town's surrender, and was refused. And since he had only 700 troops left, too few for an effective attack, Arnold had no choice but to wait for the other colonial column to arrive. Making camp just outside town, he was joined on December 2 by Montgomery and his 300 troops. When Carleton arrived from Montreal, meanwhile, he had 1800 British Regulars and Canadian militia to defend Quebec.

Together, Arnold and Montgomery launched a two-pronged assault on the city shortly after midnight on the morning of December 31, during a snowstorm. Arnold attacked from the north along the St Charles River, and Montgomery moved from the west along the St Lawrence. At Lower Town, Montgomery encountered a series of Canadian breastworks, and was killed during the attack. The colonial troops halted.

At Sault au Matelot north of town, Arnold was wounded in the leg, and command fell to Captain Morgan. Morgan's attack broke through the Canadian barricades and entered the streets of Quebec City, but, with Montgomery's attack stalled, the Americans were now cut off by the Canadians and surrounded inside the town, and Morgan was forced to surrender. (He was later released in a prisoner exchange.)

Battlefields Park, Quebec City

The fighting had cost the colonials 60 killed and wounded and over 400 captured (about one-third of their entire force), while the British had lost only 25 casualties.

After the Battle of Quebec, Arnold tried to lay siege to the city, but he didn't have enough troops, and in May 1776, when British General John Burgoyne arrived with 4000 fresh redcoats from England, the Americans retreated back to New York. The invasion of Canada came to an end.

Today, the site of the fighting is part of Battlefields Park, established in 1908 as Canada's first national park. There is a visitor center and a network of trails covering

240 acres, and a variety of cannons from various time periods on display. Much of the Park is focused on the Battle of Abraham Plains which took place on this same spot during the earlier French and Indian War.

Moore's Creek

February 27, 1776

North Carolina

The Battle of Moore's Creek, while involving just a few thousand men, was an important one, frustrating the British war plans. It was also notable for being fought entirely by Americans—both sides consisted of local militia. It illustrates the reality that the American Revolution was, in many ways, a civil war between colonists as well as a war between America and England.

While the rebellion was centered mostly in the northern colonies, the Americans recognized that they needed to defend the southern colonies as well, particularly the ports. So Washington dispatched General Charles Lee to assume command of the rebel forces in the important city of Charleston SC, one of the largest trade centers in the south. Lee had several thousand militia available, and a small cannon battery, known as Fort Sullivan, protected the entrance to the harbor.

The British also had their eye on the Carolinas and Charleston. The deposed Royal Governor of North

Carolina, Josiah Martin, had been pleading with the British Government to send troops, asserting that his colonists had been coerced into rebellion and would flock to the Royalist banner if a force of soldiers appeared. And so, believing that he would be supported by a large Tory population, General Henry Clinton made ambitious plans for an amphibious attack on the coasts of North and South Carolina with about 3,000 troops. The strategy was to pacify North Carolina and restore Royal authority there, recruit more local Loyalist militia, then move on to Charleston.

Martin now reclaimed the title of Royal Governor and issued a call for the formation of a Loyalist militia. In response, about 1600 men assembled at the town of Cross Creek, modern-day Fayetteville. Consisting mostly of Scottish-Americans who had emigrated to the area and commanded by General Donald MacDonald, a British Army officer who had been with the redcoats at the Battle of Bunker Hill, the regiment became known as the Royal Highlands. It set out from Cross Creek intending to rendezvous with General Clinton's fleet at the port city of Wilmington NC.

The rebels, meanwhile, had formed a unit of their own, the 1st North Carolina Regiment of the Continental Army under the command of Colonel James Moore. As MacDonald's Highlands left Cross Creek, Moore was able to place his 1000 men across the road as they approached: both sides issued a demand for the other side to surrender, but rather than delay his march with a confrontation, MacDonald went around the colonials and continued towards Wilmington.

Now, the rebel commander knew, MacDonald would have to cross the bridge at Moore's Creek, and while his Continentals would not be able to reach it in time, Moore sent word ahead to Colonel Richard Caswell with 800 militia and Colonel Alexander Lillington with 150 more.

At first, Caswell tried to block the Loyalists at Corbett's Ferry on the Black River, but again MacDonald found another place to cross, and Caswell fell back to Moore's Creek.

As MacDonald's force approached the bridge on February 26, Caswell and Lillington were waiting for him on the other side of the river. Not knowing how many colonials there were, MacDonald planned an attack on the rebels, but then unexpectedly fell ill. So the assault would be commanded by Lt Col Donald McLeod. As McLeod advanced, he came upon the deserted remains of Caswell's camp on the near side of the bridge—which the rebels had intentionally abandoned to make the Loyalists think they were retreating in panic. McLeod expected to meet only a small force.

The bridge at Moore's Creek

At dawn, McLeod led a group of about 500 of his militiamen, most armed only with swords, towards the bridge. It was a trap: when the Loyalists got there, they found that the bridge's wooden planks had been pulled up and they were unable to cross. Caswell's men then fired a single deadly volley from their muskets and from several field guns. McLeod and 70 of his men were killed or wounded, and the rest of the Royalists broke and ran.

The American position in front of the bridge

Now Caswell ordered his men forward. Quickly replacing the wooden planks, they swarmed across the bridge and into the Highlander's camp. Some 850 of the Loyalist militia were captured, and the rest of them melted away into the woods. Only one rebel was killed.

It was the end of organized Royalist power in North Carolina. Governor Martin once again went into exile, and the rebels now had complete control.

At the end of the Revolutionary War, portions of the Moore's Creek battlefield, located about 20 miles from Wilmington, were preserved by private citizens who purchased much of the land. In 1926 this became a National Military Park run by the War Department, then was turned over to the National Park Service in 1933. It was designated a National Battlefield in 1980.

There is a one-mile walking path that follows the road taken by the Highlanders up to a reconstruction of the bridge, and on to the remains of the Patriot earthworks, with interpretive signs and monuments including a memorial to the Royalist commander McLeod and the grave of John Grady, the only rebel killed in the battle. The Visitors Center has a small display of artifacts.

Fort Sullivan

June 28, 1776

South Carolina

After the Loyalist defeat at Moore's Creek, British General Henry Clinton cancelled his planned North Carolina landing and milled about offshore with his fleet, waiting several weeks for reinforcements from England to arrive, to be commanded by General Charles Cornwallis. They were delayed by weather, and it wasn't until May that the British ships finally anchored.

With these fresh troops at last arrived, Clinton continued on to Charleston, reaching the city on June 4 and putting troops ashore on one of the islands in the harbor. Over the next three weeks, in several skirmishes, the redcoats found themselves pinned down and unable to move, partly because one of the shoals they had planned to advance across proved to be too deep to ford even at low tide.

Clinton then decided to force his way into the harbor by bombarding and destroying Fort Sullivan with his naval force. On June 28, the cannonade began. The British had over ten times as many cannons as the American defenders, but the Fort was solidly built from sand and palmetto logs, and withstood the bombardment. The American cannons managed to damage several British ships, and three of the besieging warships ran aground in the shallow shoals. Two of these were refloated: the third was burned to prevent its capture.

During the 13-hour bombardment, a cannonball shattered the flagpole from which the rebel flag (consisting of a white crescent on a blue field) was flying, and it fell to the ground outside the fort's walls. Since lowering one's flag was a signal of surrender, an American militiaman named William Jasper promptly jumped off the wall, retrieved the flag, and returned to affix it to the top of the parapet. Today a statue stands at Charleston Harbor in his honor.

Replica cannon battery marks the spot where Fort Sullivan overlooked Charleston Harbor

As night fell, Clinton realized that his invasion attempt had failed, and ordered a withdrawal. He had suffered over 200 casualties compared to around 30 for the Americans. Only one of his frigates remained seaworthy. Three weeks later, after making hasty repairs to their ships, the British left Charleston and sailed back to New York. They would not return to the southern colonies in force for several more years.

Fort Sullivan was renamed Fort Moultrie, after the American officer who commanded it during the attack. Abandoned after the Revolutionary War, it was rebuilt in time for the War of 1812 and the Civil War, then modernized again for the Spanish-American War. During the two World Wars, it served as a base for anti-submarine duty.

Today, Fort Moultrie is part of the Fort Sumter National Park at Charleston SC, which also contains the Civil War site of Fort Sumter. Various parts of Fort Moultrie have been restored to depict the different parts of its history, from the Revolutionary War to World War II. Sadly, there is nothing left of the original 1776 sand and log fort, but the gravesite of General William Moultrie is found next to the Visitors Center.

Independence Hall

July 4, 1776

Pennsylvania

By 1775, after the battles that followed Lexington and Concord, open rebellion was an accomplished fact. The American revolutionary forces, however, still had no single unifying strategic political goal. Some colonials simply wanted direct elected representatives of their own in Parliament; others wanted autonomy and home rule under the British Crown. It was during this time, in January 1776, that Thomas Paine published (anonymously) a short booklet titled simply *Common Sense*, which proposed the goal that only a few of the rebels had seriously considered before–independence from Great Britain and the establishment of a brand new nation.

The effect was like an atom bomb, and *Common Sense* started, virtually single-handedly, the movement for American independence. Within six months, over 100,000 copies of the booklet had been printed.

In May 1776, the Second Continental Congress assembled in the Pennsylvania State House, in Philadelphia, to decide upon the political future of the North American English Colonies. On June 7, delegate Richard Henry Lee of Virginia introduced a resolution which cut to the heart of the matter: "Resolved: That these United Colonies are, and of right ought to be, free and independent States, that they are absolved from all allegiance to the British Crown, and that all political connection between them and the State of Great Britain is, and ought to be, totally dissolved."

On June 11, after several days of sometimes-acrimonious debate, the Continental Congress decided to call a recess for three weeks before voting on Lee's resolution (to give the delegates time to contact their home states and ask for instructions). But before adjourning, they appointed a five-man committee consisting of Benjamin Franklin, John Adams, Robert Livingston, Roger Sherman, and Thomas Jefferson, to draft a formal presentation of the reasons for seeking independence, to be ready if it was needed when the delegates returned for the vote. Jefferson, at age 33, was the youngest member of the Continental Congress. Although he was an uncomfortable public speaker, he was well-known as a powerful writer, and the Committee of Five in turn appointed him to write the first draft of the declaration. He began drafting the document, working alone in his room at Market and Seventh Streets, using a small wooden writing desk that he had designed himself.

In his draft, Jefferson drew heavily upon the Declaration of Rights that had earlier been written by George Mason and adopted by the Virginia Assembly. Mason's phrase "all men are born equally free and independent" became, in Jefferson's draft, "all men are created equal"; Mason's listing of "natural Rights" as

"Enjoyment of Life and Liberty, with the Means of acquiring and possessing Property, and pursuing and obtaining Happiness and Safety," became Jefferson's, "inalienable rights" of "Life, Liberty, and the Pursuit of Happiness." Surviving pieces of Jefferson's draft pages show that he wrote several different drafts and made many crossed-out changes to his text.

Independence Hall

After two weeks, Jefferson showed his final draft version to Franklin and Adams, who suggested a few more changes and then submitted it to the Continental Congress. On July 1, the Continental Congress reconvened, and on July 2, 1776, 12 of the state delegates voted to accept Lee's resolution for independence (New York did not vote—it had not yet received instructions from its assembly). Jefferson's draft Declaration of Independence was then presented to the Congress.

Over the next two days, the delegates made over 80 changes to the text in Jefferson's draft, shortening it by about 25%. One of the changes was to add the words of Lee's resolution ("These United Colonies are, and of right ought to be, free and independent States"). In deference to the delegates from the southern states, a section of Jefferson's draft condemning the King of England for allowing slavery in the colonies was dropped. (And the political impasse over slavery between the north and south would itself lead directly to Civil War less than 100 years later.) After all these changes, the delegates voted on July 4, 1776, to adopt the Declaration.

But this was not the written copy of the Declaration of Independence that was signed—in fact the Declaration of Independence was not signed at all on July 4. Instead, after the vote, the Committee of Five was directed to have copies of the document printed and distributed to the various colonial Assemblies, Committees of Correspondence, and Continental Army commanders. Some 200 copies of the Declaration were made by Philadelphia printer John Dunlap—today only 26 of these survive. One copy was delivered by horse to Easton PA, where it was read in the Circle at the center of town on the morning of July 8, the first public reading. Later that same afternoon it was read in Philadelphia. The next day, the Declaration was read in New York City, provoking an enthusiastic crowd to pull down a nearby statue of King George III.

On July 9, the New York state assembly finally sent in its official vote to accept the Lee resolution for independence, and ten days later Congress ordered that a formal copy of the Declaration of Independence be written. This appears to have been done by Timothy Matlack, an assistant to the Continental Congress Secretary Charles Thomson. Matlack copied out the final draft of the Declaration in large print onto parchment.

On August 2, 1776, the formal handwritten document was ready for signing. The first to sign was John Hancock, the President of the Continental Congress — according to legend, he made his signature extra large, saying "Now John Bull can read this without his spectacles". It is this copy, not the draft written by Jefferson, which resides today in the rotunda of the National Archives.

Jefferson's desk

In all, fifty-one delegates of the Continental Congress signed the Declaration on August 2, 1776. Five more delegates were absent, and signed later. Two delegates — John Dickinson and Robert Livingston (who was one of the Committee of Five that had drafted the document)-- refused to sign, saying that it was premature to break off relations with London and they still hoped yet for a political reconciliation. One of the signers, Robert

Stockton of New Jersey, was arrested later in 1776 by the British and, after months in jail, recanted his signature and declared allegiance to England.

Nine of the signers subsequently died before England formally recognized the independence of the United States in 1783. Jefferson and Adams, the members of the Committee of Five who had drafted the Declaration, both served as President of the US, and both died on the same day, July 4, 1826 — the 50th anniversary of the document's approval by Congress. The last remaining signer, Charles Carroll, died in 1832 at the age of 95.

Today, the Pennsylvania State House in Philadelphia where the delegates debated and voted for self-determination is known as Independence Hall. In 1787, the Hall also served as the site of the convention that wrote the US Constitution. In 1816 it was sold to the City of Philadelphia and in 1948 became part of the federal Independence National Historic Park, along with the Liberty Bell and Benjamin Franklin House.

In 1825, Jefferson gave the desktop that he used to write his draft of the Declaration to his granddaughter Eleanora Randolph Coolidge. The Coolidge family donated it to the US Government in 1880, and today it is on display at the Smithsonian Museum of American History in Washington DC.

Long Island

August 27, 1776

New York

In March 1776, General Washington, using cannons that had been captured at Fort Ticonderoga, surrounded Boston and forced the English to withdraw. British General William Howe retreated all the way to Halifax, Canada.

But Washington knew that Howe would be back, and that his most likely target would be New York City—and this would be difficult to defend. The city was the largest in the colonies and the most important trading port. But many of its merchants had extensive commercial ties to England, and Loyalist sentiment was widespread. The Revolution was not popular here. And although the city itself was at this time limited to the southern tip of Manhattan, it was surrounded by other islands that offered the British good landing spots. Defending it all would stretch Washington's little army thin—and he had no navy.

Political considerations, however, made it vital to defend the city. Until now, the colonial rebellion had largely centered in Boston, and it was necessary to demonstrate that the rebels could extend their reach beyond Massachusetts. The loss of one of its premiere cities would send the message to France and other European nations that the American rebellion was weak and unable to assert itself. New York was also a strategic place: from here, the British could send troops anywhere along the North American coastline.

And so, although Washington knew that defending New York would be very difficult, he began setting up positions to protect it. A cannon redoubt was placed at the lower tip of Manhattan (today's Battery Park), and construction was also begun on a series of wooden stockade forts. Two of these were particularly important: Fort Washington, on the New York shore of the Hudson River, and Fort Lee on the other side. Their guns commanded this stretch and prevented any British warships from sailing up the Hudson.

Another force of 9,000 troops was placed along Brooklyn Heights on nearby Long Island. In all, Washington had about 20,000 Continental Army troops and militia to defend the city.

The British government in London, meanwhile, had decided on a massive show of force. General Howe departed Halifax with 22,000 troops. His brother, Admiral Richard Howe, set sail from England with another 10,000 — the largest force that would be dispatched during the entire war. They all gathered on Staten Island in June 1776, and within two months they were ready to move. On August 22, the Royal Navy ships began ferrying troops from Staten Island to Long Island.

The American General, Israel Putnam, placed his troops along Brooklyn Heights, protecting three passes which traversed the hilly terrain. But Putnam had not done sufficient reconnaissance, and he had left another gap, Jamaica Pass, undefended.

On August 27, Howe attacked. It was the largest number of troops engaged in any revolutionary war battle. As a force of Hessians was sent against the center of Putnam's lines to tie them down, Howe sent another group of his troops pouring through Jamaica Pass to outflank the Americans. After a period of heavy fighting, including pitched fights at Battle Hill and Battle Pass, the rebels were forced to withdraw.

Historical marker at Prospect Park

The only escape route for the colonials was the Mill Dam Road, which crossed a bridge and passed through a low-lying swampy area. Here, at a position centered on the Old Stone House, a unit of 400 militia from the 1st Maryland Regiment fought a desperate rearguard action, losing 250 casualties but buying enough time for the rest to withdraw. By that afternoon the rebel troops were pressed against the East River with no way to get across. A British attack now would have killed or captured them all.

But the attack did not come. General Howe, assuming that the colonials were trapped and remembering the tremendous losses that he had suffered the last time he had launched a frontal assault against the Americans (at Bunker Hill), decided instead to surround them and force their surrender through a siege. The next day, August 28, the British began digging trenches.

Washington seized his chance, and at nightfall, in a drenching rain, he organized a flotilla of small boats to stealthily cross the river and carry all his troops back across to Manhattan. According to tradition, Washington himself was the last man to step off Long Island onto a waiting riverboat. When Howe woke up the next morning, he found that the "trapped" colonial force had disappeared. It was a brilliant tactical withdrawal by the Americans.

Washington had lost about one-fifth of his forces on Long Island. But in his evacuation he had saved some 8000 troops and kept his army intact.

Today, nearly the entire battlefield has been swallowed up by the streets of New York City. There is a monument in Greenwood Cemetery, part of Battle Hill. A reconstruction of the Old Stone House has been erected in Byrne Park, where the Maryland regiment made its stand. There are also several markers in Prospect Park, which was then part of Battle Pass.

Bushnell's Turtle

September 6, 1776

New York

After the defeat at Long Island and the withdrawal to Manhattan, Washington was desperate for a way to strike back at the British Navy and break the blockade. So he turned to a new contraption he had heard about that was secretly being built by a man named David Bushnell.

Bushnell, a student at Yale, had been working on a way to explode a black powder bomb underwater to attack ships. Although he called his device a "torpedo", it was more like a forerunner to the modern naval mine: it consisted of a wooden keg with 150 pounds of black powder, a clocklike apparatus connected to an ordinary flintlock firing mechanism to act as a timer, and a waterproof fuse to detonate the explosive. After a few months, he had perfected a reliable device. Now, he needed a good way to deliver it.

Working in secret in Connecticut with funding from the Continental Army, Bushnell and his brother Ezra constructed a one-man submarine. The odd-looking craft was made from wooden planks steam-bent into shape to form two domed ovals that were held together with iron hoops, like a flattened beer barrel. The hull measured 7.5 feet tall and 6 feet across, and was just thick enough in the middle for a man to fit inside. The whole thing was waterproofed with a layer of pine pitch. Because its shape looked like two side-by-side tortoise shells, Bushnell called his contraption the *"Turtle"*.

A cutaway replica of Bushnell's Turtle

Everything inside the *Turtle* was hand-operated. The operator (Ezra) climbed inside through a waterproof hatch in the top, and sat on a wooden bar. There were two hand-cranked propellers: one of them drove the *Turtle* forward and backward, and the other raised or lowered it in the water. A tiller operated a rudder at the back for steering. The bottom of the *Turtle* was filled with 200 pounds of lead ballast that kept it upright in the water. To make the *Turtle* submerge, a pair of hand pumps would pull water in from the outside, flooding the bottom of the compartment (and submerging the operator up to his waist). To surface, the pumps would push the ballast water back out.

Navigation came from a single compass. Since the instruments could not be seen in the dark when submerged, the needles on the dials were covered with bioluminescent fungus to show their positions. (These stopped glowing if the temperature dropped too low, so the *Turtle* could not be used during the winter.) A cork floating in a tube gave a crude measure of depth. Since there was no air pump, the operator could only submerge for short periods (about 30 minutes) until he began to run out of air and had to resurface.

To attack an enemy ship, the *Turtle* would stealthily approach the target on the surface and make its way alongside, then submerge. A pointed iron bar would make contact with the target's wooden hull, and would be hand-cranked to screw it in securely. This bar was connected by a short length of rope to the "torpedo", so when the *Turtle* withdrew, the mine remained attached to the target ship's hull. Hours later, the clockwork timer would light the waterproof fuse and detonate the explosive.

By the time Admiral Howe's fleet entered New York Harbor in 1776, the *Turtle* had undergone a series of successful tests (some of them witnessed by Benjamin Franklin) and was preparing for an actual combat mission. But, unexpectedly, Ezra Bushnell became sick and was no longer able to act as the submarine pilot. So a volunteer militiaman named Ezra Lee was recruited and hastily trained to take his place.

On September 6, 1776, the *Turtle* was ready for its first mission. The selected target was the frigate HMS *Eagle* — Admiral Howe's own flagship. At 11pm Ezra Lee climbed into the *Turtle*, and began slowly making his way out into the harbor to the anchored ship.

He successfully made it to the *Eagle* and stopped alongside her, completely undetected by the lookouts. Carefully submerging, he then moved underneath the ship and came up to the bottom of the hull. But when he tried to attach the underwater mine, he had a problem. Naval ships of this time were made of wood (usually oak), and over time they became infested with marine organisms such as barnacles, shipworms and burrowing clams, which not only increased the drag and slowed the ship, but also weakened the hull over time. To prevent this, the hulls were regularly coated with a mixture of beef fat, sulphur and pine resin, to kill the organisms and prevent new ones from re-attaching. But the British Navy had recently begun a new treatment, in which flat copper plates were attached to the underwater portions of the hull. The smooth copper not only prevented organisms from attaching themselves, but gave less friction in the water and produced a noticeably increased speed.

In the *Turtle*, Lee now tried twice to screw the mine onto the *Eagle's* hull, but both times he hit the copper hull plating, and his hand-cranked screw was not able to penetrate it. Tired, cold, wet, and running out of breathable air, he had to abandon his mission and wearily paddled back to shore. The world's first submarine mission would be unsuccessful.

Well, not *entirely* unsuccessful…

After Lee and the *Turtle* surfaced and headed toward shore, the sun was just coming up, and a group of British sailors on a nearby island happened to spot the weird-looking thing and rowed out to investigate it. To lighten his load and to distract his pursuers, Lee now armed the mine and cut it loose, and the British sailors, not knowing what it was, quickly retreated back to shore. As the *Turtle* made it to safety, the loose mine now floated around in the harbor until its detonator went off, and the 150 pounds of black powder ignited in a loud explosion that rocked the harbor. American Army officers watching from shore heard the blast and thought the *Eagle* had been successfully hit—they did not learn until later that the mission had failed.

The British intelligence network already had collected bits and pieces of information about Bushnell and his strange underwater craft, and eventually they pieced the story together. And although the attack had been a failure, the British Navy apparently took the threat seriously, and reportedly began to keep their warships far enough away from shore where they thought they would be out of reach. This had the unexpected beneficial side effect for the colonials of reducing the accuracy of the British shore bombardments.

The *Turtle*, meanwhile, was transported to the Hudson River after the fall of New York City, where it made two more unsuccessful attempts to attack British ships near Fort Lee. The submarine was then lost when a British shore battery sank the ship that was transporting it down the Hudson.

David Bushnell remained with the Continental Army for the rest of the war, and continued his work on explosive devices. Washington himself praised Bushnell's *Turtle* as "an effort of genius". In one incident in January 1778, Bushnell released a number of floating mines down the Delaware River towards the British fleet, causing minor damage to one ship. It became known as "The Battle of the Kegs". After the war Bushnell was placed in command of the US Army Corps of Engineers at West Point.

In recent years a number of functional replicas of Bushnell's *Turtle* have been built, most for use as props in movies or TV shows. In one odd incident, a performance artist in New York built a one-man sub from plywood and fiberglass, based on the *Turtle's* design, and paddled it next to the *Queen Mary 2*—and was arrested by the Coast Guard.

A replica of the *Turtle* is on display at the USS *Intrepid* Museum in New York. Another, with cutaway sides to show the internal mechanisms, is exhibited at the US Submarine Force Museum in Groton CT.

Harlem Heights

September 16, 1776

New York

After withdrawing his troops from Long Island, Washington gathered them together in a defensive position at Harlem Heights on Manhattan and awaited the inevitable British attack. He knew he was in serious trouble: his forces were not only incapable of defeating the larger British army, but many of the colonials were raw militia and were unreliable in battle. On September 8, Washington sent a frank report to the Continental Congress concluding that it was unlikely he would be able to hold New York City.

British General William Howe, assuming that the colonials were all but beaten, now extended an olive branch. Through a released prisoner, Howe sent word to the Continental Congress that he was willing to use his political influence to ask Parliament to repeal its previous taxes and to allow the colonies to live under their own elected legislatures within the British Union. After some debate about whether to respond at all to the proposal, the Congress decided to send a small committee, including Benjamin Franklin, to meet with Howe on Staten Island. But the talks quickly fell apart, as the Americans now insisted that no peace negotiations could proceed until Britain had first agreed to recognize the independence of the colonies.

Howe now proceeded to continue his move against New York City, and launched his attack on the morning of September 15. The Royal Navy, commanded by Admiral Richard Howe, carried out a fierce preliminary bombardment at Kip's Bay which drove most of the colonials' two brigades of militia away, and General Howe's troops landed virtually without a shot. By evening the British held most of southern Manhattan.

Knowlton's Rangers plaque, Columbia University

Washington stood firm on Harlem Heights. It was a good defensive position and he knew he could hold it against an attack—if his militia didn't break.

On the morning of September 16, Washington sent out a strong patrol of Connecticut Rangers to find the British. They had gone less than a mile before they ran into enemy pickets, and a group of about 300 British light infantry charged at them. It was a mistake. The Rangers made a fighting withdrawal, and the redcoats impetuously followed them almost to the American lines.

Realizing that the British had advanced too far from their own positions and were now vulnerable, Washington launched a quick counterattack. Sending about 150 militia to advance in front to hold the enemy in place, he dispatched the Rangers and some troops from the 3rd Virginia regiment, led by Lieutenant Colonel Thomas Knowlton and Major Andrew Leitch, to circle around the redcoats and attack them from behind.

But the British held their ground, and both Knowlton and Leitch were killed in the fighting. The redcoats moved up reinforcements, and so did Washington. By afternoon, some 5000 British troops were engaged with some 1200 Americans, and the redcoats had been pushed back a short distance to the top of a nearby hill, then had retreated again to a nearby buckwheat field. But neither side had intended for a major battle, and after two hours of combat, the British, running low on ammunition, pulled back to their previous lines. Washington, knowing he was outnumbered, did not follow. The redcoats had lost about 400 casualties: the colonials around 100.

To Washington, the most important result was that his militia units had stood firm and had not run. But strategically, the Battle of Harlem Heights did not alter his situation. The encounter was at a standoff: Washington's defensive position was too strong for Howe to successfully attack, but the Americans were also in no condition to drive off the much larger British force.

For the next several weeks, the lines did not move. Washington had assumed that the cannons at Fort Lee and Fort Washington would be able to prevent the Royal Navy from sailing around behind them, but on October 9 two British frigates successfully got past the forts. Taking advantage, on October 12 Howe moved most of his troops to Throg's Neck and threatened to cut off Washington's supplies and surround him. Anticipating this move, the colonials had already burned the bridges here. But with the failure of the two forts to safeguard them from the British ships, the colonials were in a position they could no longer defend. So, with Howe now temporarily unable to reach him, Washington abandoned Harlem Heights, withdrew from New York City, and retreated to White Plains.

Most of the fighting in Harlem Heights took place in what is now the heart of New York City, between present-day Broadway and Riverside Drive from 106th to 125th Streets. All of it is now gone, buried under streets and skyscrapers. The hill where the British made their stand is now the location of the Columbia University campus, and a memorial plaque to Lt Col Knowlton and his Rangers can be found there on the Mathematics building.

Valcour Island

October 11, 1776

New York

In the first years of the Revolutionary War, one of the biggest impending strategic dangers to the American rebels were the British forces in Canada, which could potentially sweep down, cut off the cities of Boston and Philadelphia from the rest of the colonies, and crush the rebellion. To prevent this, the Continental Congress decided on a daring and bold move–American forces would invade Canada first and engage the British forces there, preventing them from entering the colonies. The invasion failed, however, when the colonial forces were beaten at the Battle of Quebec, and were forced to withdraw back to Ft Ticonderoga, on Lake Champlain in New York.

Now, it was the British who saw their chance, and they poured troops across the border, led by General Guy Carleton. Since Lake Champlain was the major transportation route in the area, both sides realized that whoever controlled the lake would control the colony of New York, and in early 1776 both sides began building a fleet of warships on Lake Champlain–the Americans at one end of the lake and the British at the other. American General Horatio Gates placed General Benedict Arnold in charge of building the fleet. Arnold, who had been wounded in the Battle of Quebec, had once been a ship's captain and therefore had some naval experience. The American fleet, built in just 15 weeks, consisted of 15 ships, including several sloops and schooners and 8 gunships. One of these was christened *Philadelphia*.

The Philadelphia *on display at the Smithsonian Museum of American History*

The *Philadelphia* and her sister gunships were 53 feet long, 15 feet wide, and had a crew of 44 sailors. Designed for lake conditions, the boats were flat-bottomed with a single mast and a bank of rowing oars. The desperate Americans used whatever guns they could find, and the

Philadelphia was armed with a 12-pounder cannon at the bow, two 9-pounders on the sides that were almost 100 years old, having been made in Sweden in the late 1600's, and eight swivel guns mounted to the gunwales. She was originally designed to have a heavy "mortar" cannon at the rear, but the mortar exploded during testing. The rear of the *Philadelphia* then had to be heavily ballasted to counter the weight of the bow cannon.

On October 11, 1776, the two fleets met off Valcour Island and fought for control of Lake Champlain. General Arnold commanded the American fleet, and the *Philadelphia's* commander was Captain Benjamin Rue. The British had built a much larger fleet–25 ships to the American's 15.

Cannon from the gunboat New York *which exploded during the battle*

The battle started off badly for the Americans. As the British ships approached, Arnold sent two of his ships to meet them—and both ran aground. After some maneuvering, the two sides formed lines of battle and began blasting at each other.

Just before sunset, the British ship *Inflexible*, with 22 guns, finally arrived after a delay. It was a turning point, as *Inflexible's* guns opened up on the already-battered Americans. The *Philadelphia* was struck by a British cannonball that punctured her side and broke several of her support timbers. She quickly sank. Overnight, Arnold withdrew the remains of his fleet to the south: one by one, as the sinking vessels could no longer keep up, they were run aground, stripped of equipment, and burned. When the last American ship still afloat—the *Congress*—was also intentionally burned, Arnold and the remaining sailors marched along the lake shore to the Fort at Crown Point, where he found four small ships that had somehow escaped the British pursuers. After destroying the Fort so the British could not use it, Arnold and his men retreated to Ticonderoga. The American fleet had been almost completely destroyed.

Though the British had won control of Lake Champlain, however, it was too late in the year for the redcoats to begin a land campaign in New York. As a result, the British entered their winter camps. By the time British forces under General John Burgoyne were able to launch their campaign along Lake Champlain into New York in the spring of 1777, the American Continental Congress had already been able to raise and train enough volunteers to strengthen its own army—a feat made possible only because of the delay forced onto the British Army by the *Philadelphia* and the rest of the fleet at the Battle of Valcour Island.

After the battle, the *Philadelphia* sat upright on the bottom of Lake Champlain for 150 years and was preserved by the cold oxygen-less water. Diver and salvage expert Colonel Lorenzo Hagglund found her wreck in 1935. Hagglund recovered hundreds of artifacts from the hulk, including dishes and utensils, buttons, buckles, preserved leather shoes, 55 cannonballs, and human bones. He then lifted the entire wooden remains of the ship, with the 24-pound British cannonball that had sunk her still embedded in the planking. A number of other sunken ships have also been identified at the site of the battle, including the gunships *Spitfire* and *New York*, and the schooner *Royal Savage*.

For the next 25 years, the wooden hull of the *Philadelphia* was put on display at various sites around Lake Champlain. In 1961, the *Philadelphia* was donated to the Smithsonian, where she was restored and went on display in the Museum of American History in 1964. She is the earliest still-existing ship of the US Navy.

In 1991, a team of researchers constructed a replica of the gunboat, which they christened *Philadelphia II*. That reproduction is now on display at the Lake Champlain Maritime Museum in Burlington VT, which also has an exhibit of recovered relics from other ships in the American fleet, including a cannon from the gunship *New York* which exploded while being fired during the battle.

White Plains

October 28, 1776

New York

After the battles at Long Island and Harlem Heights, Washington realized that New York City was lost. He had always known that geography and a largely unsympathetic population would make it almost impossible for him to hold the city. But now, in the same way that political considerations had driven him to occupy and defend New York, political considerations also dictated his response to losing it. Though his ragtag revolutionary army was in no shape to stand against the British in open combat and defeat them, Washington recognized that it did not need to: the American Revolution was a political conflict, not a mere military one. As long as Washington could keep a sizable force in the field, the rebellion remained alive: his army did not need to win—it only needed to avoid being encircled and captured. And throughout the New York campaign, Washington was showing himself to be a master of the strategic retreat.

With New York City now in the hands of General William Howe, Washington withdrew his army (except for a garrison of 3,000 troops that General Nathanael Greene had, against his better judgment, convinced him to leave at Fort Washington) to White Plains about 20 miles north, where the Continental Army had a supply dump. Howe followed him, hoping to cut off the colonials, surround them, and end the war. Here, Washington formed a defensive line that was anchored on several hills near the Bronx River. He would fight a delaying action, giving him time to load and carry supplies before withdrawing further.

White Plains Battlefield Park

When Howe reached the American position on October 28, he sent a force of 4,000 Hessians under Colonel Johann Rall to attack Chatterton Hill, at the extreme end of Washington's line. Washington, seeing the advance, sent the Connecticut 2nd Regiment out to meet them. The Americans were pushed back to Chatterton Hill, and when the Hessian advance bogged down there, both sides sent in reinforcements and a fierce fight quickly developed.

Under fire from Howe's cannons and another attack by the Hessians, some of the militia units then panicked and fled, leaving the hill vulnerable. More English troops poured in, and at about 5pm the colonial line broke. British artillery could now be moved up to Chatterton Hill and would command most of the American lines, making them impossible to hold.

Chatterton Hill

But the delaying action had accomplished what Washington intended. In the middle of the night, in a driving rainstorm, Washington withdrew from the battlefield and moved towards New Jersey and the

Delaware River. He had once again escaped encirclement by a superior force, made an orderly withdrawal instead of suffering a disastrous rout, and his army (and the revolution) still survived intact. On November 1, when the rains stopped, the British at White Plains advanced—only to find that the colonials were all gone.

Howe now took part of his force and turned back towards New York City, intending to attack Fort Washington. He left the remainder of his troops under the command of General Charles Cornwallis, with orders to continue to pursue the American army.

In 1926, the White Plains battlefield was placed under the jurisdiction of the US War Department to be preserved as a historical site, and was transferred to the National Park Service in 1933. But although the site was authorized to be made into a National Park, it never happened. The NPS put up three historical plaques, but never purchased any of the battlefield or the land around it. Houses and streets soon began to cover up the site. To protect and preserve it, local citizens and the city parks' division formed the White Plains Monument Committee in 1958 and obtained a remaining parcel of land atop Chatterton Hill. Today, this small city park is all that remains of the battleground, and historical plaques and interpretive signs mark the spot.

Fort Washington

November 16, 1776

New York

The American guns at Fort Washington and Fort Lee were intended to prevent Royal Navy ships from sailing past them up the Hudson River and into the interior of New York. Positioned on high bluffs overlooking the river, and with a line of scuttled ships forming a blockade in the water, the forts were virtually impervious to British warships. But they had been built so hastily that their land defenses were never completed. As he withdrew from Manhattan, Washington had wanted to abandon the forts, but General Nathanael Greene convinced him that Fort Washington was strong enough to resist an attack, and could still be useful in restricting British movements.

But British General William Howe thought the fort was vulnerable, and after Washington's retreat from White Plains, he maneuvered his troops back to Manhattan to take it. His plan called for a multi-pronged assault to surround the fort and penetrate its land defenses while a Royal Navy frigate bombarded it from the river. Howe knew the weak spots because a Continental Army officer had defected to the British, taking a drawing of the Fort's defenses with him.

There were about 2900 American troops inside the Fort, under Colonel Robert Magaw. Since Manhattan was abandoned and the forts now served no purpose, there was no reason to keep them, and Washington began plans to withdraw the garrison across the river to New Jersey. But now the Continental Congress stepped in, ordering Greene to hold the forts in an attempt to prevent the British from moving up the Hudson River into central New York.

Washington, Greene and about 2000 troops, meanwhile, had positioned themselves in Fort Lee on the other side of the river, but they were powerless to do anything from there to help Magaw and were reduced to the role of spectators. Howe launched his attack on November 16.

Two British columns and a Hessian force assaulted the fort on three sides. The colonials fought fiercely, but were hampered by the weak defensive works. The Hessians were delayed by the river tides, but by noon the fort was completely surrounded. According to legend, during the fighting a militiaman named John Corbin, manning a colonial cannon, was hit and killed, and was replaced at his post by his wife Margaret. She became the first of several such women in the course of the war, who all became known as "Molly Pitchers".

But the colonials were in a hopeless position. One by one, as the outer defenses fell, the Americans retreated inside. Soon some 2800 troops were crammed into Fort Washington, which was only three acres in size and had never been designed to hold that many.

By early afternoon, the Hessians sent a messenger demanding that Magaw surrender or face an all-out attack. By some accounts, they further threatened that no quarter would be given, and no prisoners would be taken.

Fort Washington plaque, Bennett Park

Washington, meanwhile, had also sent a message urging Magaw to hold out until it got dark, when he would try, as he had successfully done so many times before, to withdraw the fort's defenders across the river under cover of night. To gain time, Magaw asked the British for a four-hour truce, with which to presumably confer with his officers about the possibility of surrendering. But the Hessians, perhaps suspecting what would happen, demanded a surrender within 30 minutes. Magaw knew that his battered force could not hold out until nightfall, and he agreed to give up.

The Americans surrendered 2800 troops and 36 cannons. The British and Hessians had lost 450 casualties. Three days after Magaw's capitulation, Washington left Fort Lee and crossed the Delaware River into Pennsylvania.

Today, the entire battleground has been paved over by the streets of New York City, and the only trace of Fort Washington that remains is in Bennett Park in the Washington Heights neighborhood. A historical plaque has been placed there describing the battle, and a row of stones marks the former position of the Fort's walls.

Washington's Crossing

December 26, 1776

New Jersey

The loss of New York City was a serious blow. In London the news was celebrated: Parliament and the cabinet assumed that the war would be over soon and the rebellious colonies subdued. General William Howe was awarded the title of Knight Commander of the Order of the Bath. General Charles Cornwallis began packing his baggage for the voyage home to England. A declaration was proclaimed in New York City granting amnesty to everyone who took the oath of allegiance to the King. Many, thinking the Revolution was now doomed, complied.

Washington was forced to retreat across the Delaware River to Pennsylvania, where he found himself with fewer than 5,000 men. Moreover, most of these troops had enlisted for just a year and their term was about to expire in January 1777, and there were few new recruits to replace them. If Washington did not do something quickly, his Continental Army would melt away. What he needed above all was a victory — one that would raise the spirits of his disheartened troops, encourage them to re-enlist, and keep the Revolution alive.

The target he chose was the Hessian garrison at Trenton, 1200 men under Colonel Johann Rall. They were isolated enough that Washington could launch a raid and be gone before any British reinforcements could arrive. Washington planned his attack for the early morning of December 26, when the Germans would be unprepared and still sleeping off the effects of their previous night's Christmas celebrations. The Americans would cross the Delaware River just north of Trenton, and split into two columns to cut off the Hessians and surround them.

Monument at the Delaware River

At about 11pm on Christmas Day, just as the Continental Army had begun crossing over the river, a fierce winter storm came up. Washington decided to continue with the operation, hoping that the storm would help mask his approach and give him the element of surprise that he needed, but the driving sleet caused problems for his army. Washington had planned to cross over the Delaware at three places, but the storm made this impossible and by 4am two of his columns were still on the Pennsylvania side. He decided to march on to Trenton with the 2400 troops that had already crossed.

The Hessians, meanwhile, had already been given a warning: Loyalist spies had informed the Germans that an American force was on the way. Rall, however, assumed it was merely another of the periodic small raiding parties that were harassing his outposts, and concluded that the weather would prevent any large-scale troop movements. That night, the Hessians didn't even send any patrols out into the sleet and cold. Washington's approach was completely undetected.

Battlefield Monument, Trenton

The first indication the Hessians had was at 8am when Continental Army troops suddenly began swarming out of the woods just north of town. Roused from their barracks, the Hessians tried to form up for a counter-attack, but were crowded in by the houses and buildings of Trenton. The only available open areas were the broad boulevards of King and Queen Streets (modern-day Broad and Warren Streets), which the Americans had covered with two cannons placed on top of the hill where the two streets joined, dominating the entire town. The Americans, unable to fire their flintlocks in the wet sleet, charged the Hessians with bayonets.

The fighting was over in just 90 minutes. Only a handful of Americans had been wounded, including Washington's cousin, Captain William Washington, and Lieutenant (and future President) James Monroe. The Hessians lost 20 killed and 100 wounded (including Colonel Rall, who was shot dead while trying to rally his men). Around 1,000 Hessians surrendered, along with their muskets, supplies and cannons.

While not amounting to much in the sense of military effect, Washington's raid on Trenton was nevertheless a brilliant tactical victory. More important, it provided a much-needed morale boost to the Continental Army, led to new enlistments, and kept the Revolution alive both politically and militarily. It became one of the most famous battles of the war, and the painted image of Washington crossing the ice-choked Delaware in an open boat is now one of the iconic images of American history.

Today, two separate state parks commemorate Washington's Crossing, one on each side of the river in Pennsylvania and New Jersey. In 1895, the Bucks County PA Historical Society erected a stone marker on the banks of the Delaware where Washington's raiders had departed, and in 1917 the State of Pennsylvania established the 500-acre park. On the New Jersey side, the park consists of 400 acres, with a wildlife trail and the Johnson Ferry House, which stood on the site in 1776.

In Trenton NJ, the Battle Monument is located downtown at the junction of Warren and Broad Streets, on the spot where the Continental Army cannon battery was located during the fighting. It was designed by the same architect who built Grant's Tomb, and was erected in 1892-1893. Nearby is the Old Barracks Museum, where the Hessians were quartered. It is one of the few remaining buildings left from the time of the battle. The Barracks is open for guided tours.

Princeton

January 3, 1777

New Jersey

In his original plan, Washington had hoped to launch a quick raid against the British forces in Princeton after successfully striking the Hessians at Trenton. But the bad weather, along with the stranding of half his army at the Delaware River, forced him to retreat back to Pennsylvania after the Trenton raid, taking his captured supplies and prisoners with him.

As soon as the weather cleared, though, Washington re-crossed the Delaware with 5,000 militia and Continental Army troops and re-occupied Trenton. On January 2, 1777, he was confronted by the British General Charles Cornwallis, with 5,500 Regulars.

Cornwallis posted a series of pickets between the colonials and the Delaware River and, assuming he had Washington trapped, made plans to attack in the morning. But once again Washington demonstrated his genius for strategic withdrawal: leaving behind a small force to keep all the campfires burning as a disguise, he pulled out his entire army. But, instead of withdrawing to the river as Cornwallis had expected, Washington marched around the flank of the British camp towards Princeton. When Cornwallis awoke on the morning of January 3, he found the American camp in front of him empty, and Washington's forces in his rear area. Taking advantage of his local superiority in numbers, Washington launched an attack against the rear reserve of Cornwallis's army, 1200 troops led by Lt Col Charles Mawhood.

The Battle of Princeton began somewhat accidentally, when Washington sent a detachment under General Hugh Mercer to destroy a bridge. These forces unexpectedly encountered Mawhood's troops, and a fierce fight broke out in an orchard along the road. Mercer was killed, and the Americans formed a defensive position on the top of a nearby hill.

Mercer memorial

As reinforcements from both sides moved in, heavy fighting broke out. The Americans, supported by fire from a cannon battery commanded by Captain Joseph Moulder, pushed Mawhood's troops back into a retreat.

Moulder's battery, where Colonial troops rallied

As Mawhood's forces retreated, colonial troops pursued him along the road into Princeton. But as the remnants of the British rear guard gathered around nearby Princeton University, Washington received word that Cornwallis's main forces were now approaching. Knowing that he was not strong enough to take them on, Washington broke off the engagement and withdrew, establishing his winter quarters in nearby Morristown. Cornwallis did not pursue him, but turned away and went into his own winter camp at New Brunswick.

The Battle of Princeton cost the British about 300 casualties, and about 70 for the Americans. But once again the primary effect of the battle was political: after being pushed out of New York City in apparent defeat, Washington had demonstrated that his army could still successfully attack the British, had won two battles at Trenton and Princeton, and, as the Revolutionaries gained new support, pushed the English out of New Jersey and back into New York City. The American Revolution, which had looked all but dead, was now very much alive again.

Much of the original battle site is now preserved as Princeton Battlefield State Park, established in 1989 near the city of Princeton NJ. The park also contains the Clarke House, built in 1772, which served as a temporary hospital during the fighting. Several miles of nature trails wind their way around the battlefield.

The nearby Princeton University and the Institute for Advanced Studies privately own another portion of the battleground. In 2016, the Institute announced plans to build new faculty housing on the Maxwell Field, a part of the battleground which was not incorporated into the Park. The announcement provoked opposition from preservationist groups, and the Civil War Trust raised $4.5 million to purchase the land so it would not be developed. In the end, the Institute agreed to give the land to the Park and accept a different parcel of land in exchange.

Fort Ticonderoga Siege

July 6, 1777

New York

In the spring of 1777, British General John Burgoyne was convinced that he was about to win the Revolutionary War and end the American rebellion.

After the retreat of Washington's forces from New York City (and despite what they considered to be minor skirmishes in Trenton and Princeton), the British were in a comfortable position. They now had a large force in New York under General William Howe and two more in Canada under General Barry St Leger and General Guy Carleton. The British had beaten the Americans in the naval battle at Valcour Island, but were then delayed by the onset of winter.

Now, however, as spring campaigning weather set in, Burgoyne, who had recently replaced Carleton as the British commander in Canada, formed a plan to crush the American rebellion. Burgoyne was a flashy commander and a playwright with impeccable manners, earning him the nickname "Gentleman Johnny". Under his plan, his British forces would move down Lake Champlain and along the Hudson River, while the forces under St Leger would swing around and drive east through the Mohawk River Valley. Howe, meanwhile, would take his army from New York City and march west. They would all meet up at Albany. Together, the grand combined army would overwhelm anything the Americans could put into the field, and could easily cut off Boston and Philadelphia from the southern colonies in the Carolinas, capture those colonies (which were seen as being more pro-British), and then force the rebels in the north to capitulate.

And so, when the Canadian force under Burgoyne set out in June 1777, one of its first targets was the American garrison at Fort Ticonderoga, on the western shore of Lake Champlain.

Cannons at Fort Ticonderoga

The American commander there, Major General Arthur St Clair, knew the British would attack as soon as the weather permitted, and, considering Fort Ticonderoga as the primary position defending the entire Hudson Valley, he had spent the last few months strengthening his defenses. The Fort's walls were repaired and strengthened, and additional cannon batteries were placed along the lakeshore. A floating pontoon bridge was constructed entirely across Lake Champlain, which both served as an easy route to get from one side to the other, and prevented any British shipping from passing the Fort. A strong cannon redoubt was placed on the summit of Mt Independence and several other surrounding hills.

Crucially, however, one mountaintop was left undefended: Mt Defiance, on the Lake's opposite shore, was, St Clair concluded, too steep for anyone to get cannons on top, so no gun battery was placed there. Although Fort Ticonderoga was widely viewed by the colonials as an impregnable fortress, the failure to fortify Mt Defiance would prove to be a fatal mistake.

The British reached Fort Ticonderoga on July 1, captured a few of the outlying outposts and, lacking enough men to attack by brute force, planned a siege. Examining the terrain, the British artillery officers immediately saw that the summit of Mt Defiance dominated all of the American cannon positions as well as the Fort itself. Explaining to the General that "any place a goat can go, a man can go—and any place a man can go, he can drag a gun behind him", the British artillerists succeeded, over the course of the next few nights, in hauling two heavy cannons up the side of the mountain. When General St Clair woke up on the morning of July 6, he was completely shocked to see a British flag flying from the summit of Mt Defiance and

British guns pointing directly at him, ready to pound his Fort to pieces.

Hastily convening a council of war, St Clair decided that Fort Ticonderoga was now indefensible. That night under cover of darkness he packed a fleet of small boats with his 3,000 troops and as much equipment as they could carry, and ferried across the lake to escape. When the British soldiers arrived, they found only a detachment of four Americans left behind as a rear guard—they had discovered a barrel of port and gotten falling-down drunk.

Mt Defiance overshadowing Fort Ticonderoga

The surrender of Fort Ticonderoga—virtually without firing a shot—was a severe blow to American morale. Rumors flew that General St Clair had turned traitor and had been bribed by the British to surrender the Fort—to clear his name, St Clair demanded that he be given a court-martial and was later acquitted. While this was going on, the American commander-in-chief for New York, General Philip Schuyler, was replaced by General Horatio Gates.

Burgoyne and his 8,000 troops, meanwhile, continued south. Flushed with his victory at Ticonderoga, he had no idea that his careful plan was already unraveling.

Today, Mt Defiance, on the Vermont side of Lake Champlain, is a part of the Fort Ticonderoga Museum. There is a small park at the summit, which overlooks the Lake and the Fort.

Oriskany

August 6, 1777

New York

Oriskany was an interesting Revolutionary War battle for several reasons. In terms of percent of troops engaged, it had the highest casualty rate of any battle in the war. It also illustrated a fact that is often forgotten about the Revolutionary War: it was essentially a civil war. At Oriskany, there were barely any British troops at all: on one side were Hessians and Mohawks allied with the British Crown along with units of Loyalist militia from the local area, and on the other side were colonial militias, also from the same area. Many of the opponents knew each other: indeed, at a crucial point in the battle the issue was decided because the combatants recognized their own neighbors amongst the approaching enemy. For some—including the colonial commander—it was, literally, brother against brother.

At the outbreak of the war, the Continental Congress recognized the need to defend the Mohawk River Valley, a strategic waterway in upper New York. So in 1776 a garrison of 800 colonial troops was assigned to occupy and rebuild the old Fort Stanwix, left over from the French and Indian War and located near present-day Rome NY. In early 1777, Colonel Peter Gansevoort was given command of the Fort.

When the Canadian General Barry St Leger, himself a veteran of the French and Indian War, set out to clear the Mohawk Valley as part of Burgoyne's New York campaign in July 1777, Fort Stanwix was one of his prime objectives. He reached it on August 2. St Leger had a mixed force—a small group of British Regulars, a regiment of Loyalist American militia, a number of Canadian militia, and some Hessians. On the way, he was joined by several hundred Iroquois allies (mostly Mohawk and Seneca) under the leadership of the war chief Thayendanegea, known as Joseph Brant. All together, he had about 1800 men. But with only his four small field cannons, St Leger was unable to penetrate the Fort's walls, so he surrounded it and began a siege, hoping to either starve the Americans into surrender or perhaps work his small guns into trenches close enough to the walls to be effective.

When word of the British encirclement at Stanwix reached the American General Nicholas Herkimer, he gathered a force of 800 New York militia, a wagon train of supplies, and a group of Oneida Natives as scouts, and set out to reinforce the Fort. Herkimer had served in the French and Indian War and had been a New York militia Colonel before being commissioned as General by the Continental Army. The Revolution had divided the Herkimer family: his brother was a member of one of the American Loyalist militia units marching with St Leger.

On August 5, Herkimer and his reinforcements were ten miles away from the Fort, near the Oriskany Creek. Here Herkimer halted and sent messengers to the Fort, ordering Gansevoort to send out an attack and fire a signal shot with his cannon as he did so: Herkimer planned to send his own troops in and catch the British in between.

But by the early morning of August 6 there was still no signal from the Fort (unknown to Herkimer, his messengers had not yet reached them). As the Americans in Herkimer's column grew more and more impatient, rumors began to circulate: perhaps the loyalty of the commander with the Tory brother was open to question. Herkimer seems to have responded impetuously to these whispers: as if to demonstrate both his loyalty and his bravery, he immediately gathered up his troops, formed them in column, and set off down the trail toward Fort Stanwix, with himself at the head.

The ambush spot at the bridge

When St Leger heard from his scouts about the approaching Americans, he realized that this was the sort of warfare that his Iroquois allies were best at, and he asked Joseph Brant to set up an ambush. The Native warriors chose a spot where the trail crossed a small bridge in a ravine, with thick woods on both sides. At about ten that morning, the American column reached the bridge, and the Iroquois warriors, concealed in the dense forest, opened fire.

The spot where the wounded commander Herkimer directed the battle

The first volley was devastating. In the front of the column, several American officers and around a dozen troops were killed. Herkimer fell off his horse, shot through the leg. The Third Battalion, at the rear, had not entered the ambush but heard the volley: in a panic, they broke and ran back along the trail.

But many of the New York militiamen were veterans of the French and Indian War, and now it showed. Without waiting for orders, they immediately formed up and counter-attacked into the ambush, driving the Iroquois back. A short distance away from the ravine, the Americans regrouped atop a hill and formed a defensive circle. The wounded Herkimer was carried there and, propped against a tree, continued to give orders and direct the defense.

The hill where the Americans formed their defense

Hoping to win the day through trickery, a unit of American Loyalists turned their green uniform coats inside out to try to appear as Patriot militia, gambling that they would be able to come within reach of the colonial lines. But some of the rebel militiamen recognized the approaching men as their own Royalist neighbors, and, with the ruse having failed, the "Tories" were fired upon and driven off.

While the Iroquois were masters of ambush and infiltration, their style of warfare was not well-suited to attacking a large force in a covered defensive posture. At Herkimer's direction, the American militia fought in pairs, with one soldier reloading his musket while the other aimed and shot, allowing them to keep up a steady fire. The Iroquois took heavy losses. At one point a pouring rain came up, dampened everyone's gunpowder, and forced a temporary halt to the fighting.

After six hours of skirmishing, though, the Iroquois melted away, and without them, the remainder of the British forces also gave up their attack and withdrew. Everyone's losses had been heavy: the Americans had over 450 casualties, and the British forces over 150, mostly among the Iroquois. Herkimer was carried to his own house, which was not far away, to have his leg amputated, and died from infection ten days later.

When Joseph Brant's remaining Iroquois returned to their camp, they found that a detachment of troops from inside Fort Stanwix, finally hearing from Herkimer's messengers and taking advantage of the absence of a large proportion of the British forces, had raided the Native lodges and destroyed most of their supplies and equipment. Disgusted with their losses and with the apparent lack of British ability to take the Fort, the Iroquois left and went back to their villages. They would spend the rest of the war in raids against the Oneida, who had fought against them at the battle (though in 1780, Brant would lead another group of Iroquois to try to capture Fort Stanwix, but failed).

After the battle at Oriskany, St Leger kept up his siege of Fort Stanwix for another two weeks until, learning that another larger relief force under General Benedict Arnold was approaching, he decided to abandon his efforts and withdraw all of his forces back to Canada.

Both sides claimed a tactical win at Oriskany: the British had prevented the Americans from reinforcing Fort Stanwix and had inflicted heavy casualties, while the Americans successfully drove the British forces off the battlefield and then drove them away from the Fort. But strategically, Oriskany was a boost to the colonials. The Iroquois focused on their own civil war with the Oneida and, although they launched a series of raids against colonial settlements in Pennsylvania and Ohio, the Native Americans never again played a major supporting role for the British. St Leger's withdrawal from New York, meanwhile, meant his troops would not be meeting up with Burgoyne, and would not be available when "Gentleman Johnny" needed them the most.

Today the Oriskany battlefield is a State Historic Site and a National Historic Landmark, located in upstate New York near the city of Rome. A stone obelisk was erected at the site in 1884. A walking trail with interpretive signs winds around the area, and a small Visitors Center displays maps and artifacts from the battle.

Bennington

August 16, 1777

New York

After his easy win at Fort Ticonderoga, things got more difficult for British General John Burgoyne. As he advanced towards Albany, the rebels in New York skillfully slowed his advance by felling dozens of trees across the roads — made even more effective by the huge wagon train, containing everything from officer's families to personal baggage, that trailed behind the British army. Burgoyne's progress was slowed to a crawl, and his supplies steadily dwindled as his logistics lifeline to Canada got longer and thinner.

Then Burgoyne received a stunning shock: General William Howe, whom he had expected would meet him in Albany with his army, sent a message informing Burgoyne that he would not be in New York, but was instead taking his army south to capture Philadelphia — a city of virtually no strategic importance. Burgoyne fumed at this, but under the divided British command structure, he had no authority over Howe and was powerless to do anything about it. With this one message, Burgoyne's entire carefully-crafted battle plan was no more, and he was now alone in the middle of enemy territory, with no hope of reinforcement and with his supplies rapidly running out.

But, over-confident in his assessment both of his own abilities and those of his enemies, Burgoyne did not turn back. Instead, he decided to no longer depend upon his supply line to British Canada and to begin living off the enemy's own territory, foraging for food and other supplies and, where possible, taking them from the rebels themselves. And so, on August 11, 1777, Burgoyne sent a detachment of 800 of his soldiers, mostly Hessians, a few Loyalist militia, and some British sharpshooters, all under the command of Lieutenant Colonel Friedrich Baum, to capture the colonial supply depot at the nearby town of Bennington.

It was a serious intelligence failure. The latest information obtained by the British was that the Bennington supply storehouse was protected by only a few hundred men. In reality, there were 1500 New Hampshire militiamen there, under General John Stark.

When Baum reached Bennington and found out how many troops he was actually facing, he sent messengers back to request reinforcements, and then formed a defensive position on a hill to wait for them. Stark also sent out a call for help. For the next day and a half, heavy rain prevented any action. Finally, on August 16, the weather cleared.

At around 3 in the afternoon, the Americans launched their attack. In the thick woods, they had virtually surrounded the Hessians, and now they poured up the hill. The Loyalist militia quickly broke ranks and ran, and the Iroquois scouts followed. The Hessians bunched together at the top of the hill and, when their ammunition wagons were destroyed by the colonials and they began running low on gunpowder, they made a desperate foot charge with sabers to try to break out. Baum was killed, and the Hessians soon surrendered. The fight had taken about two hours.

The position of the New Hampshire militia regiment

But, just as the Americans were gathering up their surrendered prisoners, the Hessian reinforcements arrived—550 men under Lieutenant-Colonel Heinrich von Breymann. They charged up the hill at Stark's militiamen. And then, just as the American lines began to falter, *another* group of reinforcements arrived—this time it was 350 Vermont Green Mountain Boys under Colonel Seth Warner. Now, it was the Hessians who began to waver. It was only the falling night darkness that allowed

Breymann to escape. He had lost both of his cannons and one-fourth of his men.

Battlefield memorial at the top of the hill

The battle had been a lopsided American victory. The Hessians had lost 200 killed or wounded and 700 captured as prisoners; the colonials had lost only 30 killed and 40 wounded. More importantly, Burgoyne failed to gain his desperately-needed supplies.

The Bennington battlefield is now a New York State Historic Site and a National Historic Landmark, in upstate New York near the town of Walloomsac. About 1250 acres are preserved. There are several commemorative stone markers from Vermont, New Hampshire, and Massachusetts state militia units, and a walking trail takes visitors around the battlefield.

Brandywine

September 11, 1777

Pennsylvania

We can only speculate why the British General William Howe decided, in August 1777, that he would not cooperate with General John Burgoyne's plan to meet up at Albany and attack the colonies from the north, and to take his army south against Philadelphia instead. Philadelphia was the de facto capitol of the American colonies, the place where the Continental Congress sat in session, and where independence had been declared — but in terms of military strategy it was of little value. Perhaps Howe thought that capturing the city would deal the rebellion a crippling psychological blow, reduce their will to fight, and take some of the wind out of the colonials.

In any case, ignoring Burgoyne's frantic protests, Howe loaded his 17,000 troops onto a fleet of 260 ships, sailed for the next 34 days around New Jersey, Delaware and Maryland, and finally landed at the mouth of the Elk

River in Chesapeake Bay, some 50 miles from Philadelphia. By September 10 Howe had reached Kennett Square, today a suburb of the city.

George Washington knew that the City of Brotherly Love had little military significance, but it was politically important to defend the American capitol. To oppose Howe's 17,000 redcoats and Hessians, Washington had about 9,000 Continental regulars and militia. It would be one of the largest engagements in the entire war.

Washington's headquarters at the Brandywine

Despite being outnumbered, Washington was confident he could stop the British advance, at least for a time. In order to reach Philadelphia, the British would have to cross Brandywine Creek, and there were only a few places suitable to do that. To block the redcoats, the colonials were arranged in a line on the far side of the Brandywine, covering all the potential ford sites and centered on Chad's Ford, which lay along the road where the British were marching and where Washington assumed the battle would take place.

But Washington had made a crucial mistake. In the rush to set up his defenses, he had neglected to send out a sufficient reconnaissance and did not know that there was another ford, further up the river. It would cost him the battle.

When Howe discovered that this ford was undefended, he formed a two-pronged battle plan. While half of his force, Hessians commanded by General Wilhelm Knyphausen, confronted Washington at Chad's Ford, the other half of the British army, led by Howe and General Charles Cornwallis, would slip away and cross upriver, then circle around behind the colonials and attack them from the rear. Howe hoped to encircle the entire Continental Army, trap it against the river, and destroy it.

At 5am on the morning of September 11, Knyphausen set out along the road for Chad's Ford, while Howe and his troops set out for the second ford, six miles away. Amazingly, as Knyphausen's detachment marched along, they passed a tavern where a small group of American scouts happened to be: the surprised scouts fired a few shots at the British column and then ran off to raise the alarm. Within hours, the two armies were face-to-face across the Brandywine, with Chad's Ford in between them.

Howe's plan depended on surprise for its success, and now Knyphausan did his part in the deception. To prevent Washington from noticing that half of the expected British Army was not there, Knyphausen began marching his troops back and forth from clearing to clearing and conspicuously parading his heavy baggage train around. The trick worked: the Americans had no idea that Howe, Cornwallis and 8,000 British Regulars were already on their way to cross the Brandywine and head straight for them.

The Brandywine battlefield

Late in the morning, Washington's reconnaissance network failed him again: he began receiving contradictory reports that there was a large British force on his side of the river, or that the British force was moving north away from the battle, or that the other reports were wrong and there was no British force at all. Confused, Washington first moved two of his brigades into position to block any British attack from the north, then later recalled them back to the American main lines and launched an attack across Chad's Ford at Knyphausen.

It wasn't until 2pm that the colonials received definite confirmation that there was a large British force behind them—from a local civilian who rode seven miles to deliver the news. Washington now moved several brigades to intercept the redcoats, and they were still frantically digging fortifications as Howe's troops arrived. Had Howe attacked immediately, he could have ridden through the entire Continental Army. Instead, incredibly, Howe called a halt and allowed his tired and hungry troops to eat lunch.

After finishing their tea, the English attacked, with Knyphausen's forces crossing Chad's Ford and Howe's redcoats simultaneously attacking the colonials from the right rear. Washington ordered his entire reserve, under General Nathanael Greene, to join the fray against Howe. The Frenchman Marquis de Lafayette, fighting alongside Washington, was wounded in the leg. The Americans held out for a while, but then were forced into a new defensive line about 400 yards behind. During the evening, they retreated four more times. Finally the nighttime darkness ended the fighting. The battle had lasted almost 11 hours.

It had been a near-disaster for Washington. He had lost 1200 American casualties against British losses of around 600, and his lack of reconnaissance and communications had almost cost him the entire Continental Army. Once again, the future of the American Revolution was saved by its commander's uncanny ability to extract his intact army from what looked like an impossible situation, and live to fight another day.

The fate of Philadelphia, however, was sealed. As the bulk of the Continental Army withdrew, a series of small skirmishes delayed the British long enough to allow the Continental Congress to flee to the nearby town of York. Howe's troops marched unopposed into Philadelphia on September 26.

A week later, General Burgoyne would pay the price for Howe's victory, at Saratoga. And less than a year after that, in 1778, having accomplished virtually nothing, the British troops in Philadelphia would march back out of the city.

Today, most of the original Brandywine battlefield is gone, the victim of development from nearby Philadelphia suburbia. Of the ten square miles where the fighting took place, only 50 acres is currently protected as the Brandywine Battlefield Historic Park, containing one of the hills where the Continental Army camped on the night before the battle. Originally established as a state park in 1949, the battlefield was taken over in 2009 after budgetary difficulties and is now run by the Brandywine Battlefield Associates, a nonprofit preservation group.

A museum exhibit in the Visitors Center displays artifacts from the battle, and a paved roadway allows a driving or walking tour of the battlefield, including the stone Benjamin Ring Farmhouse where General Washington set up his headquarters (the original building was destroyed in a fire, and the current structure is a reproduction), and the Gideon Gilpin farmhouse, where Marquis de Lafayette and his staff were billeted.

Saratoga

September 19, 1777

New York

After the colonial win at Bennington, General Washington realized that the British General Burgoyne was now vulnerable, and began moving Continental Army units into New York, under General Benedict Arnold, to reinforce the troops there under General Horatio Gates. By the time Burgoyne reached the Hudson River in September 1777, his path was blocked by around 8,000 American regulars and militia. Burgoyne made camp near the town of Saratoga, and sent a series of messages to Howe and Clinton pleading for reinforcements.

But as Burgoyne's supply situation became increasingly desperate, he realized that he could not wait any longer for a relief force to arrive, and that he had to break through the colonials and reach Albany before his army simply fell to pieces for lack of supplies. And so, on September 19, he launched an attack.

The primary thrust was towards Freemans Farm, held by a group of American riflemen led by Daniel Morgan. As the sharpshooters picked off British officers and artillerymen, Arnold rushed more troops into the fighting. After a day of back-and-forth combat, however, it was the English who successfully managed to push the Americans out of the area. But the British situation had only become worse. They had lost some 600 casualties, while the Americans were being constantly reinforced by local militia units arriving from the surrounding areas. The redcoats quickly built a series of cannon redoubts around the farm.

Freemans Farm

The next day, Burgoyne received a message from General Henry Clinton, in New York, who intended to attack some American forts further south to draw away some of the troops around Saratoga. Burgoyne, hoping that Clinton would then be able to meet up with him and bring more troops and supplies, decided to encamp and wait.

In the American camp, meanwhile, a bitter dispute had broken out between Generals Gates and Arnold. During the fighting at Freemans Farm, it was Arnold who had been on the field, directing his troops: Gates was in the rear in his tent. But when Gates submitted his report of the battle to the Continental Congress, he exaggerated his own role and failed to mention Arnold at all—a slight that Arnold resented. When Arnold confronted Gates over it, an argument broke out and Gates relieved him of command. Arnold sulked in his tent.

By October, it became apparent to Burgoyne that Clinton would not be able to help him. With his supplies now almost gone and his men on half-rations, he called a council of war and debated options. Most of his officers wanted to withdraw back to Canada, but Burgoyne rejected that idea, declaring it "dishonorable". Instead, he decided to attack, hoping he could break through and get to Albany.

It was a hopeless plan: the British forces had been reduced to less than 6,000 men, while the American army that surrounded him had grown to almost 13,000.

The British attacked at 2pm on October 7. In heavy fighting (during which Burgoyne had his horse shot out from under him), the redcoats were driven back, and formed new defensive positions at the Breymann Redoubt and the Balcarres Redoubt. The Americans now counterattacked.

They were joined by an unexpected commander. Hearing the shooting, General Arnold, though officially relieved of command, rushed to the battlefield and took charge. In the fighting to take Breymann Redoubt, Arnold was hit in the lower leg and was seriously wounded, but under his direction the Americans had driven the British back, and by nightfall they held the redoubts. The beaten redcoats gathered together in their main camp.

Breymann Redoubt

The British situation was now hopeless. Burgoyne was outnumbered three to one, had lost most of his best officers in the recent fighting, had no supplies left, and no hope of reinforcement. On October 17, he bowed to the inevitable and surrendered his entire army.

The American victory at Saratoga would have far-reaching effects.

Burgoyne returned to England in disgrace, and although he angrily blamed Howe for the disaster, he was never given another command in the British Army. In London, popular opinion began to turn against the war, and the Whig faction began agitating for a negotiated peace. The Cabinet soon offered a peace proposal to the Continental Congress, repealing all the taxes and laws which had provoked the conflict and offering the colonies self-rule under their own elected legislatures within a British Commonwealth. Such a policy would, in 1775, have prevented the war to begin with: now, it was simply too late.

In Paris, Saratoga convinced King Louis XVI that the American rebellion now had a chance of winning. Although the French had been sympathetic to the colonial rebels (who were after all fighting against France's longtime enemy), Louis was reluctant to openly support them. Within weeks of the victory at Saratoga, however, the French Court had worked out a formal military alliance with the American colonials to fight the English, and France would begin supplying money, weapons, and troops in North America. (A year later, the Spanish would also enter the fight against England.) It would mark the turning point in the Revolutionary War.

Through his dispatches from the battle, General Gates became a hero in the colonies. Emboldened by this, he attempted, through some behind-the-scenes political maneuvering in the Continental Congress, to have General Washington removed as commander in chief and have himself appointed instead. But when Gates was placed in charge of the American forces in the southern colonies, his spectacular failures in South Carolina led to his dismissal.

Although Benedict Arnold also won praise for his role in the battle, he felt that he had been unfairly slighted by Gates and by the Continental Congress. When he was later passed over for a promotion, his resentment grew even further, and he defected to the British, offering to turn over the American garrison fortress at West Point. When the conspiracy was discovered, Arnold fled to the other side and became a British General. And so now in the US, despite the important roles General Benedict Arnold played in the early years of the Revolutionary War, his name is synonymous with "traitor".

Today the Saratoga battlefield is run by the National Park Service as the Saratoga National Historical Park, located in upstate New York north of Albany. Established as a state park in 1927, the site was transferred to the NPS in 1938. It contains four square miles of terrain which preserves much of the battleground. Just outside the park boundaries is the restored house of General Philip Schuyler, who fought in the battle.

The Visitors Center contains displays and interpretive exhibits. There is a walking trail that takes visitors to the central parts of the fighting, including Freemans Farm and the Redoubts, and a longer driving trail that covers most of the battlefield. One of the more unusual monuments is "The Boot", a relief carving of a Continental Army leather boot with the inscription, "In memory of the 'most brilliant soldier' of the Continental Army who was desperately wounded on this spot." The un-named "most brilliant soldier" is General Benedict Arnold. According to legend, when Arnold once asked a captured colonial prisoner what he thought the Americans would do to him if he were captured, he was told they would honor his wounded leg, and hang the rest of him.

Paoli

September 21, 1777

Pennsylvania

After the Battle of Brandywine, Washington withdrew most of his army towards the supply center at Reading PA. The British General William Howe was also short on provisions, and he stayed at Brandywine for several days until he could be replenished by wagon train.

As Howe departed for Philadelphia, however, Washington saw a chance to inflict some damage on the British rear guard, possibly even destroying their baggage train. Leaving General "Mad Anthony" Wayne at nearby Chester PA with 1500 Pennsylvania militia, he directed another 2000 Maryland militia under General William Smallwood to meet up with Wayne. Together they would ambush the redcoats as they passed by. On September 19, Wayne was just two miles away from the British, awaiting Smallwood's arrival, at the little town of Paoli.

But this area had a large proportion of Loyalists who were passing intelligence information on to the British, and, unknown to Wayne, Howe knew where he was and what he was up to, and, seeing a chance to cut off and destroy part of the colonial forces, sent General Charles Gray and 1800 redcoats to attack the rebels. Gray took every step to insure surprise: his troops captured and held every civilian they met along the road (so nobody would run ahead and alert the Americans), and his men had unloaded all their muskets (so no accidental shots would give them away as they moved into position). By 1am on September 21, the redcoats reached Wayne's camp, near the Paoli Tavern.

Paoli Battlefield Park

The British charge took the colonials completely by surprise. Most of the American militia had no bayonets, and the redcoats swarmed around the camp virtually unopposed. Wayne and a small force managed to withdraw towards the nearby White Horse Tavern. The

British pursued, and unexpectedly ran into Smallwood's militia who were camped nearby on the same road. Oblivious to the presence of Howe's troops, Smallwood's inexperienced militia were unprepared for battle, and the British overran their camp and captured many of them too.

Paoli burial site

Though in terms of number of troops engaged the fighting at Paoli was just a skirmish, it was one of the most lopsided British victories of the war: the colonials lost over 250 killed, wounded and captured, while Howe's forces lost only 10 men.

Most later colonial accounts called it the "Paoli Massacre", with claims that the British infantry had bayoneted a large number of prisoners after they had surrendered, but there is no real evidence of that having happened. The recoats had captured 71 of the surprised colonials.

Wayne found himself under blame for the disaster, and demanded a court martial in order to clear his reputation. He was criticized for some tactical errors, but was acquitted on all charges.

In 1817, a stone monument was erected at the Paoli burial site, and was replaced in 1877. Today, the area is preserved by the Paoli Battlefield Site and Parade Grounds, 40 acres of which is owned by the nearby town of Malvern PA: the cemetery is run by the nonprofit Paoli Memorial Association. The battlefield is listed on the National Register of Historic Places. The site also contains a World War One monument and World War Two memorial.

Liberty Bell Shrine

October 1777

Pennsylvania

In 1777, things looked bleak for the fledgling United States of America. The rebel leader George Washington had lost at the Brandywine Creek near Philadelphia, the city was about to be occupied by the British Army, and the Liberty Bell in Independence Hall, where the Declaration of Independence had been adopted, looked like it would be captured and likely melted down to make British cannons.

Then, the Liberty Bell was saved by a wagon trip . . .

In 1751, the city of Philadelphia needed a new bell. In those pre-communications days, city governments called their citizens together with the ringing of a bell, whether to pass on important proclamations and announcements or to gather the local militia and citizens in response to some threat or danger. When the new Pennsylvania State House building was completed to serve as the capitol for the colony, the colonial government sent to London to have a new bell cast. The new bell was, the officials specified, to be of 2,000 pounds in size, and to have the inscription "Proclaim Liberty thro' all the Land to all the Inhabitants thereof.-Levit. XXV. 10". The bell arrived from London in August 1752, was eagerly placed on a wooden stand and rung to test the sound—and cracked. City officials tried to return the bell to London to have it re-cast, but the ship that had brought it didn't have enough room to take it back.

Two local iron founders, named Pass and Stow, offered to re-cast it, though they had never made a bell before. They broke the London bell into pieces, melted them down, added a bit more copper to the bronze to make it less brittle, and then cast it into a mold. When the bell was delivered in March 1753, city officials publicly tested it. This time it didn't crack, but instead of a proper bell ring, it made an odd clanging sound. Pass and Stow, mocked by the crowd, sheepishly took the bell back to their shop, melted it down, added some tin, and re-cast it again. This time, the bell seemed acceptable, and it was hung in the steeple of the State House in June 1753.

Over the years, the bell was rung to call the State Assembly together, to call public meetings and militia musters, and also on special occasions such as (in a wonderful historical irony) the ascension of King George III to the British throne in 1761. According to later mythology, which may or may not be true, as the colonies became more rebellious, the bell was also rung to call citizens together for heated public discussion of the Sugar Act in 1764 and the Stamp Act in 1765. By 1775, however, and perhaps earlier, the steeple in the State House was beginning to deteriorate, and the bell was no longer rung, as it was feared the wooden tower might collapse.

Liberty Bell

In 1775, at Lexington and Concord, the American Revolution broke out. On July 4, 1776, the Declaration of Independence was adopted by the Continental Congress, inside the Pennsylvania State House (which would be known afterwards as "Independence Hall"). When the Declaration was first read in Philadelphia on July 8 (not on July 4, as is commonly believed), every available bell in the city was rung in celebration—but it is not known whether the bell in the State House was rung on that day, or whether the poor condition of the bell tower prevented that. Thus, in another irony, the State House bell—destined to be known as The Liberty Bell—may not have actually participated in the event for which it is most famous.

In 1777, the British Army launched a campaign to capture Philadelphia, and defeated Washington's forces at the Battle of Brandywine. With Philadelphia now open for occupation by the British, the Continental Congress fled the city. All 11 of the large bronze bells in the city, including the bell in the State House tower, were removed, to prevent the British from melting them down and casting the bronze into cannons. The bells, along with baggage, refugees, and other items from Philadelphia, were loaded onto a 700-wagon train, guarded and escorted by 200 cavalry from the North Carolina 4th Regiment. The State House bell was in the care of a member of the Pennsylvania militia named John Jacob Mickley.

Replica Liberty Bell in Zion Reformed Church, Allentown

The wagon train made its way up the Bethlehem Pike towards the Lehigh Valley. On September 23 in Bethlehem, just four miles from their destination, Mickley's wagon broke down and he had to remain behind while the rest of the wagon train moved on. The heavy bell had to be laboriously transferred to another cart, owned by a militia member from Philadelphia named Frederick Lieser.

At least two of the bells from Philadelphia, including the State House bell, ended up at the Zion Reformed Church in Allentown, which was being used by the Continental Army as a military hospital. They were buried under the floorboards, and stayed there until June 1778, when the British troops left Philadelphia. When the bells were returned to the city, the State House bell, with its tower still in bad shape, was placed in storage until the steeple was rebuilt in 1785, two years after the United States of America won its independence from England in the Treaty of Paris. After that, the bell was rung to call the state legislature into session, and also each year to commemorate the Fourth of July and Washington's Birthday.

It wasn't until after the anti-slavery Abolitionist Movement adopted the State House bell as one of its symbols, however, in 1835, that it began to be referred to as "The Liberty Bell". It was also around this time that the bell's first crack appeared. Historical sources are unclear when this happened; it may have been as the bell was being rung for the death of Chief Justice John Marshall in 1835, or sometime during the next ten years on the Fourth of July or Washington's Birthday. What is known with certainty is that officials tried to repair the crack by filling it with metal, but when the bell was rung for Washington's Birthday in 1846, the crack was enlarged beyond repair, and the bell was never rung again.

In 1848, the Liberty Bell was removed from the bell tower and placed on an ornate pedestal inside Independence Hall, where it remained through the Civil War before being hung from the ceiling in the Assembly Room. From 1885 to 1915, the bell made a number of railroad tours across the nation before returning to be displayed inside Independence Hall. In 1975, in preparation for the Bicentennial celebrations, the Liberty Bell was moved to a glass pavilion outside on Independence Mall, then to a more secure pavilion in 2003, where it remains today, as part of Independence National Park.

At Zion Reformed Church in Allentown is a "Liberty Bell Shrine" which displays a replica of the bell, and a small museum exhibit of artifacts which tells the story of the trip from Philadelphia.

Valley Forge

December 19, 1777

Pennsylvania

By the time winter fell in 1777, the American Revolution was, once again, in desperate straits. Though General John Burgoyne had been defeated decisively at Saratoga, other British troops under Generals William Howe and Charles Cornwallis still held New York City and had captured the American capitol at Philadelphia. In his winter camp at Valley Forge, on the Pennsylvania side of the Delaware River, Washington's troops were, as always, short of supplies and equipment, and the one-year enlistments of most of the Continental Army troops were about to expire in January 1778, at which time most of his army would simply go home. And this time, unlike the raid on Trenton the year before, there was no opportunity for a quick win that could spark morale, embolden the army, and entice the troops to re-enlist for another year. It was the lowest point of the Revolution. As pamphleteer Thomas Paine wrote, "These are the times that try men's souls."

The Continental Army was safe from British attack: Valley Forge had been turned into a fortress, with entrenchments and cannon redoubts all around. But the Continental Army was falling apart: desertions became so high that Washington was forced to post pickets to prevent men from leaving, and floggings (and sometimes executions) of deserters became a routine sight in camp. The General himself was under attack, as critics led by General Horatio Gates intrigued within Congress to cashier him and replace him as commander. Finally, Congress was pressuring him to launch a mid-winter attack on the British to re-capture Philadelphia—something he knew he could not do. Unless Washington dealt with the situation soon, his army would disappear, he would likely be replaced as commander, and all the hopes of the Revolution would vanish.

Cannon redoubt

It was now that Washington's subordinate officers stepped forward and saved the day. Two in particular became vital: General Nathanael Greene was placed in charge of the supply organization, and General Friedrich von Steuben was tasked with training and drilling the Continental Army. Greene managed to wrench some money from the Continental Congress and also reorganized the commissary system so that supplies could flow faster and more effectively. Although the Continental Army would always be short on supplies, its situation soon became much improved.

Von Steuben statue

The more visible improvement was brought about by Von Steuben. Throughout the war, the Continental Army's performance had been haphazard: at times the American Regulars had stood firmly in their lines and fought it out with the British, and at other times (sometimes during the same battle) they had broken and run from an English volley. Although most of the troops had received some rudimentary training in the militia, they were far from a professional fighting force, and what they needed above all was strong military discipline and rigorous training in the art of 18th century warfare. Von Steuben would provide it.

Von Steuben billed himself as a "Baron" and as a "General". He was in fact neither, but he was a former Captain in the Prussian Army who had served as a staff officer, and he had a natural talent for both organization and leadership. So when Washington appointed him to run the Continental Army's training, he picked 100 soldiers as a "model company", trained them personally, then each of those 100 would train another group of 100, and so on until the whole Army had been covered. Von Steuben also ended the practice of placing new recruits directly into active units (where they were expected to learn on their own) and began a regular program of training new arrivals as a unit. Finally, Von Steuben recognized that the one-year enlistment term was a waste of manpower, since troops would be leaving just as their training and experience was beginning to make them useful, and he pushed Washington and Congress into expanding the enlistment term to three years, or sometimes for the duration of the war.

He also imposed a uniform set of training procedures. Till now, each regiment was formed locally by its own officers, and every unit had its own set of formations, marching orders, organization, and combat steps. Von Steuben ended this, and drilled every unit in the same procedures, based on his own training manual. Known as "The Blue Book", Von Steuben's infantry manual served as the basis for US Army training until after the War of 1812.

Beginning with the step-by-step field process for loading and firing a musket, the troops were then practiced relentlessly in unit maneuvers and combat formations. And although Von Steuben drilled the soldiers every day, rain or shine, on the Valley Forge parade ground and mercilessly swore at them in German and French, the troops loved him. By the time the Continental Army left Valley Forge in the spring of 1778, it had been transformed into a tightly-disciplined force that could be counted upon to stand its ground and fight. (The local militia units, by contrast, remained unsteady and unreliable throughout the entire war.)

And perhaps most importantly, it was while encamped at Valley Forge that Washington received the news that the French, impressed by the colonial victory at Saratoga, had decided to openly join in the war and ally themselves with the rebels. The desertions stopped, enlistments shot up, and the Continental Army was reborn. Soon a flow of weapons, supplies, and eventually French troops would make its way to America.

In 1893, Valley Forge was established as Pennsylvania's first State Park. Run originally by the Valley Forge Park Commission, it was taken over by the Pennsylvania Department of Forest and Waters in 1923 and then the Historical and Museum Commission in 1971. On the nation's Bicentennial in 1976, the site was donated to the Federal Government by the State of Pennsylvania, and was incorporated into the National Park Service as Valley Forge National Historical Park on July 4, 1976.

The park contains 3500 acres. But because of its proximity to the King of Prussia suburb of Philadelphia, many areas of the encampment have become endangered. In 2001, a parcel of land within the campsite was placed on sale and purchased by a real estate developer, and after much effort it was bought by the NPS and added to the park. In 2007 another private landowner made plans to construct a hotel and museum within the campsite: a local citizens group was able to block the effort, exchanging the land for a piece of property within the city of Philadelphia.

Today, travelers to Valley Forge see a large Visitors Center which displays artifacts recovered from the site, and periodically has historical re-enactors and living history demonstrations. There are 26 miles of trails, which include reconstructed cannon redoubts, memorial statues, the 1917 Memorial Arch, and the stone farmhouse used by Washington as his headquarters as well as structures used to house other Continental Army officers. A number of barracks cabins used by the troops have also been reproduced. There are guided Ranger talks and trolley tours of the grounds available.

Valley Forge is one of the most-visited Revolutionary War sites in the country, with over a million tourists per year.

Monmouth

June 28, 1778

New Jersey

After occupying the city of Philadelphia in September 1777, the British General William Howe accomplished ... nothing. Meanwhile, he had come under criticism from London, where General Burgoyne was blaming him for the disaster at Saratoga. Howe, in turn, sent a series of messages back to England declaring that it was he who was being treated unfairly, blaming the Crown Government for not giving him adequate men or resources to fight the American War, and indignantly asking to be relieved of his command and sent back to England. His request was granted, and command of his army fell to General Henry Clinton. As soon as he arrived to take charge, Clinton decided to evacuate Philadelphia and march his troops back to New York City. They left on June 18, 1778.

Clinton's intent had been to march his 20,000 troops overland through New Jersey all the way to New York, but with his heavy guns, huge baggage train, and large numbers of Loyalists and civilians following him, his progress was ponderously slow, so he decided to turn northeast and make for the Jersey coast, where he could be picked up by ship. On June 28, the British Army was camped near the little town of Monmouth Courthouse.

Washington's forces, about 14,500 men, were nearby. As the British lumbered along, their baggage train stretching for twelve miles behind them, Washington saw a chance to inflict some damage on them by attacking the column's rear guard, using a detachment of 5,000 troops under General Charles Lee. As Lee moved into position, Clinton—who had expected a rebel attack—unwittingly played into Lee's hands by leaving 4,000 men of his rear guard to protect some bridges while his main force continued on to Monmouth, a few miles away. Lee now had a perfect opportunity to block the British rear guard in place, allowing Washington to approach with the rest of his troops, surround the detachment, and destroy it.

Instead, things fell apart. Lee's orders to his subordinate officers were confusing and unclear, and instead of a coordinated attack there was a disorganized rush. The British held their ground and were quickly reinforced, and Lee found himself facing a much larger force than he had expected. His 5,000 troops turned and ran.

As Washington marched with his men towards the battlefield, expecting to surround the British, he was instead shocked to see Lee's soldiers running headlong past him in the opposite direction. It was later said that this was the only time in his life that the normally-reserved George Washington swore out loud. Angrily relieving General Lee of his command and taking over himself, Washington dashed about on his horse and succeeded in halting the rout, gathering up the retreating troops and organizing them into a defensive line near the Craig farmhouse and some bridges. The British also paused to reorganize, then attacked at about 1pm. There was heavy fighting along a hedgerow near an apple orchard.

The Hedgerow at the Orchard

The British were halted by an American cannon position at the Perrine Farm, and Clinton quickly moved his own cannons up to deal with it. There followed four hours of nearly constant barrages from both sides.

The fighting was compounded by the weather—it was an extraordinarily hot summer day with temperatures near 100, and the troops of both sides, in their heavy uniforms, suffered from heat exhaustion. Several local women carried pitchers of water to the American gun crews during the battle, both for drinking and for swabbing out the hot barrels between shots. One of these became the subject of legend: when the husband of Mary Ludwig Hays was hit and wounded, she reportedly took his place on the cannon's crew, and became known to posterity as "Molly Pitcher".

"Molly Pitcher" Memorial

While this artillery duel was going on, however, one of General Nathanael Greene's officers, who had grown up in this area, pointed out a pathway that led to the top of nearby Comb's Hill, and Greene was able to place four American cannons there. They had a commanding view of the British emplacements and soon opened a devastating fire. Clinton was forced to withdraw back to his camp. Washington readied his troops to attack the British in the morning, but Clinton had broken camp in the night and retreated. The British had suffered about 350 casualties, against 260 for the Americans.

But the most important effect of the battle was on the morale of both sides. Not only had Washington turned around a potential rout of his own troops, but he had then gone on to push the British off the battlefield. Clinton recognized that the now-disciplined Continental Army was a much more formidable force than the ill-trained militia that the British had been facing before. In the weeks after Monmouth, some 2000 Hessians, now convinced that the war was unwinnable, deserted, melting away into the German-American populations in New Jersey, Pennsylvania and New York.

General Lee, stung by the criticism he got for his precipitous retreat in the first stages of the fight, asked for a court-martial to clear his name. Instead, he was convicted of cowardice and sentenced to a one-year suspension from command. He never served in the Continental Army again, and amid whispers that he had intentionally betrayed his soldiers to the British, he died of yellow fever in 1782.

Today the Monmouth battlefield is a State Historical Park, in central New Jersey, opened in 1978 and run by the Division of Parks and Forestry. The Visitor Center museum, opened in 2013, has a large-scale map of the battle, as well as artifacts and displays, and a network of trails and interpretive signs covers about 1800 acres of the battleground. The Craig Farmhouse and the Cobb House, scene of much of the fighting, have been restored.

In 1990, local citizens formed a nonprofit group, the Friends of Monmouth Battlefield, to organize an annual re-enactment at the site and to raise money for the purchase of land parcels to add to the Park.

Wyoming Valley

July 3, 1778

Pennsylvania

In the aftermath of the British defeats at Oriskany, Bennington and Saratoga, the Iroquois Confederation of Native Americans, most of whom had actively allied themselves with the English in hopes of stopping colonial intrusions into their territory and perhaps winning back some of their lost lands, concluded that there was little point in joining the redcoats in large pitched battles. Native American warfare had always traditionally been a matter of hit-and-run raids and ambushes, and now it was this style of fighting that the Iroquois turned to. Their target was Pennsylvania.

The Wyoming River Valley, just north of present-day Scranton, had already been the scene of conflict. The colonies of Pennsylvania and Connecticut both claimed title to the territory, and there had been a steady influx of Connecticut settlers. The Iroquois, meanwhile, also regarded the Wyoming Valley as theirs, and launched war parties on occasional raids. When the Revolutionary War broke out in 1775, the local population became separated into Patriot and Loyalist militias, influenced as much by which side they thought would support their land claims. So when the Iroquois war leaders Joseph Brant and Cornplanter planned a series of raids from the area around Fort Niagara into the Wyoming Valley in the summer of 1778, they were joined by local Loyalist militia and a unit of British Rangers under Captain John Butler. Altogether, the combined Iroquois/Loyalist force numbered about 1000. The local Continental Army commander, Colonel Zebulon Butler, had only a force of around 400 local militia.

The Wyoming Massacre Monument

On July 1, the Loyalists occupied the virtually-undefended Fort Wintermoot, near present-day Wilkes-Barre PA. The next morning, about 500 Loyalists and

Iroquois moved on to Forty Fort, which was occupied by the Patriot militia under Colonel Zebulon Butler. Colonel Butler knew that he was safe inside the Fort, but he also knew that with Washington's troops tied up in New Jersey, he had no chance for reinforcement and could not withstand a long siege. So, with little choice, he decided to move out and attack his besiegers. Butler and his 400 militia marched towards the British at Fort Wintermoot.

The British commander Captain John Butler, upon hearing that the rebel force was approaching, set up a trap. Hoping to convince the colonials that he had withdrawn, Butler ordered his own Fort to be set on fire and set up a battle line in the nearby woods.

When Colonel Butler and his rebel militia arrived that afternoon, however, they spotted the Loyalists lying in wait and, forming into a line of their own, attacked. But their advance was halted by Loyalist fire, and the Iroquois circled around behind them and swarmed out of the woods. Surrounded and trapped, the colonials were massacred. Those who tried to surrender were cut down. British reports declared, "In truth, the Indians gave no quarter," and noted that the Iroquois warriors had taken 227 scalps, with some of the captured militiamen reportedly taken back to nearby Native American villages and ritually tortured before being killed. It became known as the "Wyoming Massacre". Of the 387 colonial militia who marched towards Fort Wintermoot, only 60 or so escaped, including Colonel Zebulon Butler.

The Patriots blamed the British for the killings, and the massacre galvanized popular opinion in Pennsylvania against the Crown. A Continental Army regiment under Colonel Thomas Hartley was moved to the area and fought a few skirmishes with the Iroquois.

When the Native American raids continued in the spring of 1779, General Washington dispatched General

John Sullivan to lead a campaign into Pennsylvania and New York to eliminate the Iroquois as a threat. Washington ordered a "scorched earth" policy: "The immediate objects are the total destruction and devastation of their settlements, and the capture of as many prisoners of every age and sex as possible. It will be essential to ruin their crops now in the ground and prevent their planting more."

Sullivan left the town of Easton PA on June 18, 1779, with 4000 Continental troops and militia. The Iroquois did not have the strength to face such a force, and the only real fighting happened at Newtown, in which Sullivan smashed a Seneca attempt at ambush. By September, the colonials had penetrated deep into New York, destroying at least 40 Iroquois villages along the way. As Sullivan's troops left to rejoin Washington's army in New Jersey, the Iroquois had been crushed, their military power destroyed, and their territory reduced to ruin. Most retreated to English-held Canada. Shortly after the Revolutionary War ended, the Natives would surrender nearly all of their territory to the US in the Treaty of Fort Stanwix.

In the aftermath of the Wyoming Massacre, the bodies of almost 100 victims were buried at the battle site. In 1833 a stone memorial was erected, and the bones were reburied underneath. Today, the Battle of Wyoming Monument is owned and maintained by the Wyoming Monument Association. In 2010, the stone memorial was restored after being struck by lightning.

Fort Boonesborough

September 7, 1778

Kentucky

At the end of the Seven Years War, England recognized that it needed a buffer between its colonies along the east coast and the French territory in the west. And so in 1763 the King's Government declared a Royal Proclamation that set the border of all its North American colonies at the Appalachian Mountains, outlawed any expansion beyond that, ordered all British settlers there to return east, and prohibited the establishment of any new colony except by Royal Charter. In the former French territory between the Appalachians and the Mississippi River, Parliament planned to establish a separate province for the Native American nations that had allied with it, including the Shawnee, Cherokee and Choctaw, to be known as "Indiana". Under British protection, Indiana would safeguard the American colonies against French incursions as well as prevent border disputes between the two European powers that could lead to another war in North America.

The American colonists, however, who had not been consulted at all before this policy was adopted, objected vigorously. Many of them, particularly those like Virginia, the Carolinas and Georgia who were heavily dependent upon plantation agriculture, had always claimed all the land to their west up to the Mississippi River and were already seeking to expand into these fertile areas, and there had already been several frontier skirmishes with Native Americans as white settlers, supported by local militia, encroached upon hunting grounds claimed by the tribes.

In March 1775, a group of land speculators from North Carolina, calling themselves the Transylvania Land Company and headed by Judge Richard Henderson, crossed the Appalachians and entered the Native territory called Kan-tuck-ee. Their intention was to buy a large tract of land from the Native Americans and establish a new colony to be known as Transylvania. At Sycamore Shoals, Henderson met with the Cherokee chiefs Attakullakulla and Oconostota, and convinced them to sign an agreement granting him ownership of 20 million acres. Since the treaty violated the 1763 Royal Proclamation, it was entirely illegal, and the Royal Governors in Virginia and North Carolina both issued arrest warrants for Henderson. Further, much of the territory signed away by the Cherokee actually belonged to the Shawnee or Chickasaw.

Nevertheless, Henderson hired frontiersman Daniel Boone (who as a translator had helped negotiate the treaty at Sycamore Shoals) to scout a wagon trail through the Cumberland Gap and into "Kentucky". When this Wilderness Road reached the banks of the Kentucky River, at the site of modern-day Lexington KY, Boone and about thirty of his men built a stockade enclosure that became known as Fort Boonesborough. Within two months Henderson had joined him there, and some 100 settlers were dwelling in a series of small towns around the Fort.

Fort Boonesborough

When the Revolutionary War broke out in April 1775, the settlers in Kentucky didn't concern themselves with what was going on in faraway Boston. But Henderson did see an opportunity for legalizing his land grab, and approached the new Continental Congress with a proposal to recognize the legality of the Transylvania colony, now that the Royal Governors had been deposed. The Congress, however, decided to defer the matter to the North Carolina and Virginia Assemblies, both of which claimed the disputed territory for themselves and repudiated Henderson's treaty with the Cherokee.

At the same time, however, the Native tribes of Kentucky were making moves to expel what they saw as illegal invaders into their land. The Cherokee chief

Tsiyugunsini ("Dragging Canoe"), declared that the treaty had been illegal (though his father Attakullakulla had been one of the chiefs who signed it). The Shawnee under Chief Blackfish, meanwhile, also claimed parts of the treaty land. Both leaders now allied themselves with the British, hoping to drive the Americans out and establish a Native homeland of their own under England's protection. Supplied and armed by the Canadian Lieutenant Governor Henry Hamilton at Fort Detroit, Shawnee and Cherokee war parties launched a series of raids on the settlements in Kentucky, killing or capturing some 200 colonists.

In February 1778, Boone himself was captured by a Shawnee war party and, under Native American custom, he was forcibly adopted into the tribe. When Blackfish began planning an attack on Fort Boonesborough four months later, however, Boone escaped and gave warning. On September 7, 1778, Blackfish arrived with almost 450 warriors, mostly Shawnee but also Cherokee, Miami, Lenape, Wyandot, and a small number of Canadian militia. Boone and forty Kentucky men, with about 100 women and children, were holed up inside the Fort.

The Natives had no heavy guns and had no way to get through the stockade walls, and so a truce was declared to negotiate a settlement. After a few days, an apparent agreement was reached: the Shawnee and Cherokee would recognize white ownership of the land and withdraw to the Ohio River Valley, and in exchange the settlers in Kentucky would pledge their allegiance to the British Crown.

But as both sides gathered to sign the agreement, something went wrong. It's still not clear what happened: according to the settlers the Shawnee warriors attacked them, and according to the Natives the settlers opened fire. Boone and his men retreated inside the fort, and the siege began again. Over the next week, Blackfish's warriors tried unsuccessfully to set fire to the fort's walls. The Canadian militiamen tried to dig a tunnel, but the wet soil collapsed. In desperation, the Shawnee launched an all-out assault on the front gate on September 17, but this failed when a heavy rainstorm soaked everyone's gunpowder. The next day, Blackfish and his force gave up and left.

Although the Shawnee would continue to launch hit and run raids along the colonial western frontier, after this defeat at Boonesborough most of the British-allied Natives withdrew to the area around Fort Detroit near Canada.

In 1965, the state of Kentucky opened a State Park at the site of Fort Boonesborough, and in 1974 work was completed on a reconstruction of the fort. Erected near the actual site, the rebuilt stockade fence is twice as big as the original, and contains a number of cabins where living history exhibits demonstrate colonial frontier skills such as soap-making, candle-dipping, yarn-spinning and blacksmithing. Each September, the siege of Fort Boonesborough is re-enacted.

Vincennes

February 23, 1779

Indiana

After the withdrawal of the Shawnee and Cherokee from their unsuccessful siege at Fort Boonesborough, only one major British position remained on the western frontier. In 1777, the British had formed a small military camp on the Wabash River, on the border of what is now Indiana and Illinois, at the site of an old French and Indian War fort. The English called it Fort Sackville: the French called it Fort Vincennes after the nearby town. It was intended to defend the area against the colonials in Pittsburgh, but because it was so remote the fort was never really made effective. It served largely as a base from which to equip small Native raiding parties.

In May 1778, the Governor of Virginia, Patrick Henry, authorized Lieutenant Colonel George Rogers Clark to lead a force into the area. Spreading the news of the new French-American alliance, Clark convinced most of the local population, the descendants of French settlers, to join with the rebel cause. The remaining British retreated back to Canada, and Clark's men took Fort Sackville without a shot.

In late 1778 however, the Canadian Lieutenant Governor Henry Hamilton arrived to re-occupy Vincennes with a force of 40 British regulars, 50 French-Canadian militia, and around 200 Native Americans allied with the English—mostly Shawnee. The small American garrison surrendered in December 1778, and Hamilton immediately began strengthening the fort with reinforced blockhouses and a new stockade wall.

The only colonial force nearby was a group of 180 militia, under Clark's command, in the town of Kaskaskia, about 180 miles west of the Fort in the Illinois territory. (Around half of these were French.) Clark realized that from a reinforced base at Vincennes, the British and their Native allies could launch renewed raids ranging from New York all the way down to Kentucky. He also realized that not only did his band of militia lack the strength needed to take a fortified position, but he had no chance of being reinforced by any other colonial militia or by the Continental Army. Nevertheless, he concluded that it was best to attack the British fort as soon as possible before its defenses were completed. And so, after writing to a friend that he considered the whole expedition to be a "forlorn hope", Clark set out from Kaskaskia on February 5, 1779.

During the 18th century, virtually all military campaigning would come to a halt every winter as everybody retired to their camps. The plight of Clark's expedition illustrates why: slogging through the wet snow, his progress was painfully slow, and it was simply impossible for supplies to reach him by wagon or mule. Dependent solely upon what they could carry along with them, Clark's men took longer than expected to cover the 180 miles to the Fort and ran out of food three days before reaching their goal. They arrived cold, wet, and hungry.

But when they reached the town of Vincennes on February 23, they received a pleasant surprise: a local trader named Francis Vigo told Clark that not only were most of the local French townspeople sympathetic to the colonial rebels, but the British in Fort Sackville had no idea that his troops were approaching. The villagers in Vincennes supplied the colonials with food and ammunition.

Hoping to take the Fort by surprise, Clark immediately moved to attack. Taking advantage of cover, he was able to hide his numbers while at the same time displaying a large number of flags and also firing shots from one location before rapidly moving to another, thereby giving the British the impression that the American force was much larger than it actually was. After several hours of trading gunfire, though, the Americans were unable to get through the Fort's walls.

The next morning, Clark presented a demand for surrender. Hamilton, inside Fort Sackville, refused, but agreed to a truce to discuss terms. At this time, a war party of Native raiders was captured as they tried to slip through the American lines to the fort, and Clark decided upon a show of resolve to force the British to surrender. Releasing a number of the captives who were French Canadian, Clark took the five remaining Native Americans, bound them, forced them to kneel in sight of the Fort's walls, then had his men hack them to death with tomahawks, throwing their bodies into the nearby river.

Although the British considered the incident to be an outrage and it featured prominently in English anti-rebel propaganda, the killings had the effect that Clark intended: when he met with the British commander

Hamilton in a nearby church under a flag of truce on the morning of February 25, surrender terms were reached. Hamilton, seven of his officers and 16 British troops were taken as prisoners and escorted to Williamsburg. The remaining French-Canadian militiamen (some of whom had already refused to fight against Clark's fellow French militiamen) were paroled and marched back to Fort Detroit. Clark had managed to capture Fort Sackville without losing a single man (though several of his men died in a cannon accident afterwards while celebrating the victory). Clark renamed it Fort Patrick Henry.

With the loss of Vincennes, the British and their Native allies no longer had any effective force on the colonial western frontier, and, despite sometimes bloody raids by both sides for the rest of the war, the Americans now had undisputed control of all the land on the western side of the Appalachian Mountains, from the Ohio River Valley all the way down to Kentucky.

Memorial at George Rogers Clark National Historical Park

After the war, Fort Patrick Henry was abandoned, and as it decayed the town grew to cover it over. In 1905, the Daughters of the American Revolution commemorated the battle by putting up a stone memorial at the spot where the Fort had stood. In 1936, the Federal Government financed a monument at the spot, and it became a state park. In 1966, the State of Indiana donated the site to the National Park Service, and the monument underwent a restoration in 2009. There is a Visitors Center with artifacts from the Fort, and the monument contains a statue of Clark and a series of murals depicting the battle.

The War At Sea

September 23, 1779

England

Although the American colonies had depended since the beginning on sea trade and had a large merchant marine fleet and ship-building industry, the fledgling United States had little experience with naval warfare and no ships suitable for engaging the Royal Navy.

It wasn't until six months after Lexington and Concord that the Continental Congress authorized an official US Navy, consisting mostly of privateers—privately-owned merchant ships which were outfitted with guns and granted licenses to harass and capture British shipping. Over 2,000 British merchant ships would be captured during the war by American privateers.

But the colonies were crippled by their lack of organization. While land forces could at least be raised and equipped by state militias, a sea-going naval force required the direction of a central authority with sufficient funding and direction, and the Continental Congress was never able to fill that role. Of the thirteen new frigates ordered by the Congress in 1775, only six were completed before the end of the war. Most of the smaller ships that were built, consisting largely of 21 sloops, were either captured by the British or burned by Americans to prevent their capture.

Therefore on the whole, with some particular exceptions, the Royal Navy was virtually unchallenged by Americans throughout the war. Enjoying full naval superiority, the British were able to move their troops almost at will up and down the coast, and also carried out harassing raids on American ports with impunity. Even when Washington had the British land forces surrounded in New York City for the last half of the war, he could not launch any effective assault to drive them out because he had no ships that could contend with the Royal Navy frigates surrounding Manhattan Island.

The earliest ships that were specifically commissioned and built by the US Navy were inland, on Lake Ticonderoga and Lake Erie. Most of these were lost in the Battle of Valcour Island.

One of the first open-sea naval actions of the Revolutionary War took place in February 1776, when Commodore Esek Hopkins took a group of eight ships and a battalion of 200 Marines and raided the British port at Nassau in the Bahamas, capturing a quantity of supplies and weapons—then seized two more British merchant ships on the way back. Hopkins' fleet also encountered the British warship *Glasgow*, which inflicted some damage and then escaped.

Four months later, Captain John Barry was escorting an American merchant ship, loaded with military supplies, into Cape May NJ when two British warships closed in. Barry managed to beach the merchant vessel, unload her supplies onto his two smaller ships, blow up the now-empty vessel, and evade the British ships to deliver the supplies.

But by far the best-known naval actions of the Revolutionary War came from naval commander John Paul Jones. In April 1778, after having served as the captain of the small ship *Providence* and the 24-gun sloop *Alfred*, Jones was given command of the sloop *Ranger* and sent to attack British shipping off the coast of England. Over the next two months, operating from his base in France, Jones captured six British merchant ships and the British war sloop *Drake*, which had surrendered on April 24 after a one-hour fight.

In June 1778 France officially entered the war, and the French Navy now gave Jones command of a five-ship squadron, led by the 900-ton *Bonhomme Richard*, a captured British East India freighter which had been fitted with 42 guns. Although the fleet was under the command of the American Jones, only one of the ships, the *Alliance*, had been built in the United States: the rest had all been built or captured by the French and had French captains: their crews were a mix of Americans, French, and British prisoners who had accepted American amnesty. In the fall of 1779, Jones took the little fleet on a voyage completely around the British Isles, capturing a number of merchant ships and even attempting to blockade the port at Edinburgh.

But his most famous action came on September 23 when he encountered a British convoy of over 40 cargo ships, most carrying iron or timber, escorted by the 44-gun frigate HMS *Serapis* and the small sloop *Countess of Scarborough* off Flamborough Head in the North Sea. Jones turned his fleet to attack: the *Serapis* positioned herself between the two fleets to protect the merchant ships while the *Countess of Scarborough* first escorted them to safety, then turned to join the *Serapis* and engage the

Americans. After some maneuvering, the *Serapis* found herself in combat with the *Bonhomme Richard* and two smaller ships, while the *Countess of Scarborough* had become separated and was engaged with the American ship *Alliance*. It was just beginning to get dark.

The extra guns that Jones had added to his ship proved to be of inferior quality, and two of them exploded when fired. So he switched tactics and, instead of a long-range gunfight, decided to attempt to grapple with the *Serapis* and board her. But the *Serapis* was more maneuverable than the American ship, and continually evaded Jones. At one point, the *Bonhomme Richard* accidentally rammed the stern of the *Serapis* and her bowsprit became entangled in the British ship's rigging. With both ships temporarily helpless and unable to fire on the other, the British Captain, Richard Pearson, with remarkable humor, called out to the Americans, "Has your ship struck?", a punning reference to the act of striking one's colors in surrender. Jones, with equal good humor, responded with, "I have not yet begun to fight".

By this time, the *Countess of Scarborough* had broken off from its duel with the *Alliance* and tried to sail away from the battle: the *Alliance* pursued her. The other American ships could not fire at the *Serapis* without the danger of hitting the *Bonhomme Richard*, so they stood off.

The *Bonhomme Richard*, meanwhile, was in trouble: several cannon shots had penetrated her hull below the waterline, and she was slowly sinking. But now Jones got a stroke of luck. Once again, the two ships became entangled together, but this time Jones was able to swing his ship around, bringing her side-by-side with the *Serapis*. Jones immediately ordered his boarding party into action, and the deck of the *Serapis* was swept with swivel gun and musket fire. For the next hour, the two ships' crews fired at each other, with neither able to gain an advantage.

Then, around 9:30pm, a barrel of gunpowder ignited aboard the British ship—perhaps from an American fire grenade. The resulting explosion swept across the deck of the *Serapis*, killing or injuring dozens of crew. But still the fight continued.

By now, the *Countess of Scarborough* had surrendered to the *Alliance*, and the American ship returned to join the *Bonhomme Richard*. Here, she fired several broadsides into the locked ships, which did just as much damage to the *Richard* as to the *Serapis*. But at last the British captain Pearson realized that his position was hopeless. At 10:15pm, he struck his flag and surrendered. Jones transferred his crew to the captured *Serapis* and attempted to pump the water out of the crippled *Bonhomme Richard*, but the ship was too badly damaged and sank the next day.

Jones took the rest of his fleet and his captured prizes to port in Holland. But this produced a diplomatic problem: Holland was still formally neutral in the war and had not yet officially recognized the United States. The British issued a request that, being a person with no nation and flying no national flag, John Paul Jones was legally a pirate, and the two captured ships should be returned to England. So Jones hastily fashioned his own "naval ensign flag" from cloth scrounged up aboard the captured *Serapis*—his flag consisted of alternating red, white and blue stripes, and a blue field with thirteen stars—and asked the Dutch to recognize him as an American combatant.

The Dutch officials, not wanting to get dragged into the affair, declared that the *Alliance* was clearly an American ship, and that the American John Paul Jones was in command of it. The other ships were then affirmed to be French, and Holland had no legal obligation to hold or return any of them.

While all this was going on, a group of British warships soon gathered outside of the Dutch harbor, intending to capture Jones and the *Alliance* as soon as they left port for the United States, but Jones managed to hide his vessel inside a larger convoy of Dutch merchant ships and escape. He returned to the US as a hero.

In the end, though, Jones was of more consequence as a colonial morale-booster than any actual military result. The US Navy was small and ineffective. While it was a naval victory in Chesapeake Bay that brought about the final surrender of the British in the American colonies, it would be a French fleet, not American, which won that fight.

A Serapis flag on display at the North Carolina Capitol museum

The hastily-improvised flag that Jones flew from his captured British ship was adopted as the official "ensign", or naval flag, of the United States, and became informally known as the Serapis Flag. Today, the North Carolina Capitol Museum has a Revolutionary War Serapis Flag on display as part of its collection of historical American flags.

Savannah

October 9, 1779

Georgia

With the British surrender at Saratoga and the retreat from Philadelphia, nearly all of the northern colonies were firmly in the hands of the rebels. The British, meanwhile, were being drawn into combat with the French in the Caribbean over control of the rich sugar colonies, and the political agitation in London against the American War was growing. Things were going badly for London.

So the English Generals decided to adopt a different grand strategy: from now on, they would focus their efforts in the southern colonies. These were, they thought, not as radical as Boston or Philadelphia, and could be relied upon to produce their own local Loyalist militia troops which would assume the task of fighting against the rebels, thereby freeing up British resources to use against France.

The first target was the port city of Savannah GA. In December 1778, British Lieutenant Colonel Archibald

Campbell landed on the Georgia coast with 3,000 troops. The American commander there, General Robert Howe, had only 1200 militia troops, and although he had formed a strong defensive position on the edge of an impassable swamp, the British found a pathway through the wetlands and emerged at the rear of the colonial forces. The entire American force was captured; the British lost only 24 men. Savannah became a British base.

Campbell was soon replaced by a column of troops from St Augustine (in British Florida) under General Augustine Prevost, and the British began conducting raids from Savannah into the rest of Georgia, capturing riverways and several towns. Sir James Wright was installed as Royal Governor, and Georgia was once again under British rule. Proclamations were released granting amnesty to all who submitted to the King. But when Prevost tried to recruit new units of Loyalist militia, he got less than 2,000 volunteers. It was an ominous sign that the British had overestimated the level of support they were likely to get in the south.

The Americans, meanwhile, had a force of several thousand troops in Charleston SC under General Benjamin Lincoln, who now replaced General Howe as commander in the south, but Lincoln realized that he could not recapture Georgia without facing the Royal Navy, and the colonials had no ships with which to do that. So they turned to their new French allies for help. The French had a strong fleet in the Caribbean under Admiral Charles Comte d'Estaing, but he was occupied with the capture of Grenada and St Vincent, and was not available for several months. The planned joint French-American invasion of Savannah was delayed until September 1779.

While Lincoln marched from Charleston with 2,000 men, d'Estaing's fleet bombarded Savannah and landed a force of French artillerists. In response, the British defenders hurriedly began constructing a series of cannon redoubts. When the French commander demanded his surrender, the British General Prevost asked for a 24-hour truce to confer with the Royal Governor—during which he was reinforced by another 1,000 troops—then formally declined. The siege began.

By October, however, d'Estaing was becoming concerned about his fleet. Not only were his ships exposed to storms and hurricanes on the coast, but he did not know where the British Navy was and did not want to risk being surprised and cut off from his supply bases in the Caribbean. And so, over the objections of the American General Lincoln, d'Estaing decided to force the issue by making a land assault on Savannah with a joint force of 4,000 French and American troops, including a unit of freed Black slaves from the French colony at Haiti. Lincoln was doubtful that the attack would be successful, but since he was completely dependent upon the French, he had no choice but to agree.

Spring Hill Redoubt

The attack began just after dawn on October 9, focusing on the British redoubt at Spring Hill. This was a simple square earthenworks with a ditch and wooden abatis, armed with cannons that had been taken from several small British warships. A number of other positions surrounded it. In all, Prevost had about 3,000 men. The French had chosen the Spring Hill position because it was manned by Loyalist militia and they thought it would be easier to attack, but during the night a deserter had informed Prevost of the plan, and he had moved a unit of British Regulars to reinforce the Redoubt.

The attack faltered from the very start. Part of the French force became mired in a swamp and never even reached the British. The fire from the English redoubts was intense, and although the Americans and French managed to climb the walls at Spring Hill, they were repulsed. D'Estaing was wounded, and the Continental Army's chief engineer officer, Kazimir Pulaski, was killed. In all, the French and Americans lost almost 1,000 casualties, while the British lost around 150. The bloodiest part of the fighting, around Spring Hill redoubt, had been largely American rebel vs American loyalist.

After this rebuff, Lincoln argued that they should continue the siege, but a severe storm now hit d'Estaing's fleet. He sailed for France on October 18. Lincoln was forced to withdraw his troops back to Charleston.

Although it was one of the bloodiest battles of the Revolutionary War, the siege of Savannah had accomplished only a military disaster. But it also had political repercussions. The French and the Americans had seen each other in action—and neither was impressed. D'Estaing considered the colonial troops to be inexperienced, ill-equipped, untrained, and too apt to retreat, and was now reluctant to risk his fleet again in their support. Lincoln, on the other hand, thought that the French were imperious and arrogant, and they seemed to view the Americans as underlings rather than as equal partners. It was not an auspicious beginning to the "grand alliance".

Today, nearly all of the Revolutionary War battlefield is gone, swept away by the streets and houses of the city. The siege of Savannah is commemorated in Battlefield Memorial Park, opened in 2003, which contains a number of monuments and a replica of the Spring Hill Redoubt which was located here. In 2008, archaeologists excavated the site and portions of the original wartime trenches and walls were found. More portions of the battlefield were uncovered in nearby Madison Square and at the Jewish Burying Ground.

In the Savannah History Museum, across the street from the Redoubt, there are artifacts from the battle, recovered during the archaeological excavations. The city also has monuments to the Haitian troops who fought in the battle, to Colonial engineer Kasimir Pulaski (who was killed in the fighting), and to General Nathanael Greene, who lived in the city after the war and is buried nearby.

Castillo San Marcos

1779

Florida

One of the most forgotten aspects of the Revolutionary War is the fate of the prisoners who surrendered or were captured in battle. The British held almost 25,000 Americans as POWs during the war. Of these, as many as 20,000 died in captivity—five times as many as had been killed in combat.

At this time, it was common for European armies to subject their prisoners to "parole", an arrangement in which the captured man gave his name and residence and was then released after signing a promise that he would stay at home and not fight again in the war. It may seem to be a shockingly naive system to us today, but it actually worked pretty well—military men of that time prided themselves on their honor, and in any case the parole was enforced by the practice of checking all new prisoners against the list of previous parolees, and if a paroled prisoner was captured again, he would be summarily executed.

From the outset of the Revolutionary War, however, the British Government considered the colonials as ordinary criminals and treasonous traitors, not as enemy combatant soldiers. Under English law, they could all have been hanged for treason and sedition. Instead, captured rebels were housed in prison ships, first in Boston Harbor and then in New York. The conditions in these prison barges were notoriously horrible: there was no protection from the weather, and little food or water. As the war continued, three prisons were set up in New York City—one for officers and two for rank-and-file. Conditions here were no better. Of the 31 American prisoners captured at Bunker Hill, 20 were dead within three months, and of the 2,800 colonials who surrendered at Fort Washington, only 800 survived to be released 18 months later in a prisoner exchange. Later at Charleston, almost half of the 6,000 colonials who surrendered died in captivity.

The Continental Army protested several times to the British Government about its treatment of prisoners, and at one point Admiral Richard Howe tried to negotiate an agreement with Washington. That attempt fell victim to politics: Howe, refusing to acknowledge the legality of the American army, addressed his proposals to "George Washington, Esquire", and the Americans, asserting their independence, refused to consider any communication that was not addressed to "General George Washington". The Crown Government, meanwhile, offered release to individual prisoners if they signed an oath of loyalty and agreed to fight for the British. On some English warships, as much as one-fourth of the crew was now made up of American ex-prisoners.

On the American side, the official position at the outset was to treat the British prisoners well, in the hopes that they could be exchanged for captured rebels. But the housing of POWs was left largely up to the colonial governments, and its quality varied from place to place depending on how much money was available. The colonies also varied in their treatment of captured Loyalist militiamen—some colonies considered them as prisoners of war, while others considered them as traitors and criminals. Since the Continental Congress had few prisons suitable for holding British POWs, most of the prisoners were sent to small towns on the western frontier, where, confined by their remoteness, they were housed in churches or other public buildings and left to roam freely in town, working in farm fields or as laborers.

After Burgoyne's surrender at Saratoga, meanwhile, the Americans for the first time found themselves faced with the problem of housing and feeding a large number of English POWs. The surrender terms offered to Burgoyne specified that all his troops would be released, on condition that they all be sent back to England. But the Continental Congress balked at this and refused to approve the agreement. Burgoyne's (and later Cornwallis's) troops were all dispersed to various locations in the US and held until the end of the war.

In 1776, the British relaxed their position somewhat and adopted a policy in which prisoners from both sides could be exchanged. (This seems to have been the result of pressure from the German Hessians, who did not want to fight in a conflict in which their POWs would not be released.) But it wasn't until 1783, after the fighting in North America was largely over, that Parliament passed a law acknowledging the Americans as combatants and specifying humane treatment for the POWs.

When the war moved its focus to the southern colonies in 1779, the British needed prisons that were closer to the action, and one of the spots selected was the Castillo San Marcos, an old stone-walled Spanish fortress in St Augustine FL.

Castillo San Marcos

After the Revolutionary War, Florida was given back to Spain and then purchased by the United States in 1821. The Americans occupied Castillo de San Marcos, renamed it Fort Marion, and utilized it as a military prison and POW camp (it was one of the places where the Seminole chief Osceola was imprisoned during the Seminole Wars) until 1933, when it was given to the National Park Service. Today the site is a National Monument.

Charleston

March 29, 1780

South Carolina

After the English capture of Savannah and reconquest of Georgia, the next target was Charleston SC, the largest port in the southern colonies. Almost four years earlier, British General Henry Clinton had tried to take the city by a direct naval assault on its defenses, and had been beaten back. Now, as the French fleet withdrew from Savannah, Clinton saw his chance to try again, and this time he would surround Charleston and besiege it.

In February 1780, after a month-long voyage, 9000 British troops under General Clinton landed at Simmons Island, 20 miles down the coast, and marched towards Charleston from the land side. Washington quickly sent reinforcements of his own from New York, and the Americans had about 6000 defenders in the city under the command of General Benjamin Lincoln. Trenches were dug, and walls were made from a cement-like mixture of lime and seashells called "tabby". Things were so desperate that the Continental Congress had suggested a serious proposal to the South Carolina colonial government that they grant freedom to their large number of African-American slaves and arm them—a proposal which horrified the plantation owners and was summarily rejected.

The British advance was slowed by a series of several small skirmishes, and it wasn't until March that Clinton arrived at Charleston. Almost immediately he scored an important success: Lincoln had hoped that a shallow sandbar would prevent the Royal Navy ships from approaching close enough for an effective bombardment, but on March 20 several British ships managed to cross the sandbar and get into the harbor. Fort Sullivan (now renamed Fort Moultrie), which had so successfully fought off the British fleet in 1777, was cut off and forced to surrender.

The only remaining bit of the defensive tabby walls surrounding Charleston

At this point, General Washington would likely have retreated his force and withdrawn, as he had successfully done so many times when faced with a superior enemy. But Lincoln decided to stay and fight it out. By April 2 Clinton had occupied an unbroken string of positions around the city and opened up a nearly constant cannon bombardment. The siege had begun.

After several unsuccessful attempts to break through the British lines, Lincoln knew he was doomed: there was no way for him to be either reinforced or resupplied. On April 21, he sent an offer to Clinton to turn the city over to the English if his forces were allowed to withdraw. This offer was rejected.

Historical marker at Marion Park

A week later, the British further weakened the American defenses by draining a canal that was blocking part of their advance. The English cannons were now just

250 feet from the city's defenses. On May 9 Lincoln once more offered to withdraw and surrender the city, and this time Clinton agreed, on condition that the entire American force be paroled and not fight again until formally exchanged. Lincoln rejected those terms. But his position was now hopeless: on May 11 Lincoln reluctantly agreed to an unconditional surrender: the 6,000 defenders were held as POWs, and while the officers were later exchanged for British prisoners, the rank-and-file soldiers went to prison barges and camps, where almost half of them died. It was one of the largest American surrenders of the Revolutionary War.

With Lincoln's defeat, Clinton sailed back to New York City, leaving General Charles Cornwallis in command to continue the reconquest of the Carolinas. Cornwallis immediately issued a series of proclamations which re-established British rule in Charleston, and ordered that Royalist militia units be formed. But once again the British misjudged the mood of the population.

In the absence of any large colonial force in the region, the Americans turned to guerrilla warfare, and a number of local commanders, most importantly Thomas Sumter and Francis "Swamp Fox" Marion, waged hit and run raids against the British garrisons and their supply lines between Charleston, Savannah, and Augusta. The Loyalist militia and the British, particularly the cavalry units under Lt Col Banastre Tarleton, retaliated with strikes of their own, especially against civilians who were suspected of supporting the guerrillas. It degenerated into a confusing and vicious exchange of raids, massacres, and counter-raids. Tarleton in particular gained a reputation for ruthless brutality: by various accusations he was held to have abused civilians, burned unarmed towns, executed captured guerrillas, and killed Colonial Regulars as they tried to surrender.

The British, meanwhile, found that, contrary to their expectations, the local population was not sympathetic to them, and they found it almost impossible to organize a large Loyalist militia force. Despite the successful British invasions in Georgia and South Carolina, they were no closer to winning the war.

Today, virtually none of the fortifications and trenches from the 1780 siege of Charleston still survives—they have all been obliterated by the modern city. Fort Moultrie, which surrendered early in the conflict, is a part of the Fort Sumter National Park. Much of the fighting happened along King Street and Marion Square, but the only remaining trace of the battle is a historical marker at the spot and a piece of tabby wall, all that remains of the once-extensive defensive works surrounding the city.

Camden

August 16, 1780

South Carolina

With the loss of Georgia and South Carolina, the way was now open for British troops to advance through North Carolina and into Virginia. This was a deadly threat to the rebellion: Virginia was the largest and wealthiest of the American colonies, and was providing much of the funding, supplies, and manpower for the Continental Congress and its Army.

The task of halting the British advance was given to General Horatio Gates, still lauded as the hero of Saratoga. Landing at North Carolina with 2000 troops, Gates gathered whatever local militia forces he could, swelling his ranks to about 4000, then advanced to attack the town of Camden in South Carolina, where the British had a large supply depot garrisoned by 1000 redcoats. And in doing so he made a major mistake. There were two roads leading to Camden: one was shorter but went through Tory-held territory: the other was longer but was controlled by rebels and partisans. Gates chose the shorter route. As a result, his army arrived at Camden low on supplies, hungry, and ill with dysentery.

Learning of the American movement, British General Charles Cornwallis rushed out of Charleston with more redcoats and about 600 Loyalist militia to reinforce Camden. After joining all his forces together, Cornwallis, though outnumbered, decided to intercept the Americans as they approached. Gates got there first, but rather than attacking the outnumbered British garrison, he settled into a defensive position instead for a few days, then began to move along the Waxhaws Road to attack. He didn't know that Cornwallis was already there, moving up the same road to attack *him*. The two armies met in the dark outside Camden, along the Waxhaws Road, on the night of August 16.

The Camden Battlefield National Historical Landmark

Until then, Gates thought he was only facing the small garrison at Camden; it was only after this brief skirmish that Gates learned that Cornwallis's forces had already arrived and his 1500 Continentals and 1500 militia now faced 2000 British regulars. After considering withdrawing to a stronger defensive line at Clermont, Gates finally concluded that he would not be able to make a safe retreat and had no choice but to stand and fight it out. He planned a dawn attack.

But the British reacted first. Cornwallis sent his infantry in a bayonet charge against a formation of North Carolina and Virginia militia. Lacking bayonets of their own, the Americans broke and ran, and in minutes Gates's entire left flank had crumbled. Fearing a total collapse, Gates fled the battlefield, riding all the way to Charlotte NC.

De Kalb memorial, Camden Battlefield

A formation of Continental soldiers, meanwhile, were standing their ground against the British, but with the disintegration of the militia they found themselves outflanked and outnumbered almost three to one. Nevertheless, under the command of Gen. Johann De Kalb, the Americans resisted for over an hour before a British cavalry force swept around behind them and attacked from the rear. De Kalb was killed, and the colonials now fled the field. British cavalry under Colonel Banastre Tarleton pursued them for 20 miles. One unit of Americans, surrounded by the redcoats, tried to surrender, but Tarleton's men cut them down where they stood.

Both politically and militarily, the Battle of Camden was a disaster for the rebels. The Americans lost 1000 killed and wounded and another 1000 captured, and their army was all but destroyed as a cohesive force. The British lost about 300 casualties, but they were once again in sole control of the Carolina colonies.

When the Continental Congress heard about Gates's headlong flight from the battle, it began an inquiry, which, due mostly to Gates's extensive political connections, eventually acquitted him of cowardice. But the General's reputation was ruined and he never commanded another colonial army again. In December 1780 he was replaced as commander in the southern colonies by General Nathanael Greene. Greene immediately began the task of rebuilding a colonial military force to resist the British advance into Virginia.

Cornwallis, meanwhile, was waging a political fight of his own. In order to cripple the local plantation economy and to help raise Loyalist militia, the British General issued orders granting freedom to any African-American slave who crossed over into the British lines. In

Georgia, South Carolina and North Carolina, at least 12,000 slaves joined with the English. Some fought in Loyalist militia units: many others were sent to freedom in the Caribbean or England.

Today, part of the 2,000-acre battle site at Camden is preserved by the Battle of Camden National Historic Landmark. This was originally a 6-acre park owned by the Daughters of the American Revolution: since then it has grown to about 800 acres, much of it purchased from a nearby paper mill in 2002 and 2007. Another 800 or so acres of the historic battlefield remains in private hands. In 2015, the National Park Service studied the possibility of obtaining the area as a National Park, but concluded it was "not feasible".

Another 500 acres are preserved in the nearby Historic Camden Revolutionary War Site, a park that is managed by the nonprofit Palmetto Conservation Foundation. It has an "affiliation" with the National Park Service. The site contains an outdoors living history museum, reconstructed colonial buildings including the Kershaw House used by Cornwallis as his headquarters, and an area of rebuilt British fortifications from the battle.

Kings Mountain

October 7, 1780

South Carolina

The Battle at King's Mountain is notable for two reasons: it was the turning point for the rebellion in the southern colonies, and it was fought entirely by Americans against Americans — there was only one British soldier on the entire battlefield.

So far, the British strategy of attacking the southern colonies was, they thought, working out well; they had won three major battles and regained two of their lost colonies. After defeating the colonials at Camden and establishing control of South Carolina as well as Georgia, General Charles Cornwallis decided to move on to capture North Carolina, and marched his forces north from Charleston. By October, he had reached the town of Charlotte NC, just over the border.

One of the units that made up Cornwallis's right flank was a regiment of 1000 Loyalist militia from South Carolina, led by Major Patrick Ferguson. Ferguson had been wounded at Brandywine before being sent to Charleston and taking command of the local militia. He was a colorful character, who often roused local Loyalists into enlisting with a speech, given with his thick Scottish accent, declaring, "If you would be pissed upon by a set of mongrels, then say so, and let your women turn their backs to you and search for real men." After Camden, Ferguson had fought a number of skirmishes against guerrillas from North Carolina led by Colonel Isaac Shelby.

Now, as the British advanced north, Shelby's raiders continued to harass Ferguson's militia. Vowing to "march this army over the mountains, hang your leaders, and lay waste your country with fire and sword", Ferguson took off after them with his 1000 South Carolina militia and about 100 Loyalist sharpshooters from New York — and in the process became dangerously separated from the main British force.

Monument obelisk at the top of the mountain

The colonials saw their chance. Within days, rebel militia and guerrilla forces from all over North and South Carolina as well as a group from Tennessee under John Sevier (known as the Over-Mountain Men) had gathered near the border, hoping to trap Ferguson in his camp at Kings Mountain. Forewarned of the danger by two defectors, Ferguson made plans to break camp and move his force closer to Cornwallis at Charlotte, but the colonials picked 900 of their best riflemen, put them on horses, and rode all night in the rain to catch the Loyalists before they could retreat. They arrived at Kings Mountain on the afternoon of October 7. With its steep boulder-strewn sides, Ferguson considered the position unassailable. "Well boys," he declared to his troops, "here is a place from which all the rebels outside of Hell cannot drive us!" He was wrong.

Ferguson's gravesite

The colonials were mountain men and such terrain was no obstacle for them. They quickly ascended the hill.

Ferguson had not set out pickets or fortified his camp, and he had no idea the rebels were there until they charged up the hill, yelling "Give them Tarleton's quarter!"—a reference to the British Colonel Banastre Tarleton's brutal executions of guerrillas and his massacre of surrendering colonials. As the guerrillas poured rifle fire into them, Ferguson rallied his Loyalist militia and led a bayonet charge that drove the rebels down the hill and into the woods, where they reformed and attacked again.

On the third charge, Ferguson was killed, and the Loyalists sent an emissary with a white flag. For several minutes, until their officers could stop them, the rebel militia continued to pour bullets into the Loyalist ranks, killing many of those who were trying to surrender (including the bearer of the white flag). The entire Loyalist force was killed, wounded, or captured.

Fearing a counter-attack by Cornwallis's nearby force, the rebels then hastily gathered up their prisoners and left. Along the way, they placed some of the captured Loyalists on "trial" for offenses during the guerrilla campaigns, and at least nine of them were summarily hanged. Within a few days, however, most of the Loyalist prisoners escaped or were paroled and released as the colonial militiamen, with no means of holding them, dispersed and went back into North Carolina.

Upon hearing of the defeat, Cornwallis abandoned Charlotte and withdrew back to Charleston SC. With the destruction of the South Carolina militia at Kings Mountain, he had lost almost a third of his entire force. The British were confined to their strongholds in Charleston and Savannah, and the entire southern countryside now belonged to the rebels.

For almost a century, the Kings Mountain battlefield lay forgotten. There was a commemoration in 1855, and a stone monument was dedicated in 1880 on the 100th anniversary. In 1899 the Daughters of the American Revolution raised money, bought the battlefield land, and dedicated a stone obelisk memorial in 1909.

In 1930, President Herbert Hoover gave a speech at the site on the 150th anniversary of the battle, and in 1931 Congress established the Kings Mountain National Military Park. Today the Visitors Center has an interpretive film and exhibits, and a 2 mile paved trail takes visitors around the battlefield to several monuments and memorials, including Major Ferguson's grave. The military park is also located next to the Kings Mountain State Park, a wilderness area with extensive nature trails and campsites.

Mobile

January 7, 1781

Alabama

When the Seven Years War ended in 1763, one of the treaty requirements was that Spain turn over control of her North American colony in Florida to the British. When the thirteen colonies declared their independence from England in 1776, Florida, now sometimes called "The Fourteenth Colony", remained firmly Loyalist, under Royal Governor Peter Chester.

British Florida was divided administratively into two parts. The peninsular portion, known as East Florida, was governed from St Augustine. The panhandle portion, which at that time also included the cities of Natchez, Baton Rouge, and Mobile along with the capitol at Pensacola, was known as West Florida.

After France joined with the American rebels and declared war on England, the Spanish Empire also saw an opportunity to win back some of its former territory—including Florida. So in September 1779, after Spain's entry into the war, Col. Bernardo de Galvez, the Governor of Spanish Louisiana, captured the city of Baton Rouge, then set sail from New Orleans in January with 800 troops to invade Mobile.

Reconstruction of Fort Charlotte

After being hit by a hurricane on the way (and nearly abandoning the effort), Galvez's fleet landed near Mobile and, after receiving about 400 reinforcements, began the attack on March 1, 1780. The British commander, Elias Durnford, was holed up in Fort Charlotte with less than 300 troops. To provide fields of fire and deny cover to the attacking Spanish, Durnford burned most of the buildings in town.

The Spanish in turn began bombarding the Fort on March 10. Durnford knew that a British relief column was on its way from Pensacola, and tried desperately to hold out until it arrived. But the Fort's walls were breached by Spanish artillery two days later, and Durnford surrendered after a brief infantry fight.

Galvez's next target was Pensacola, but when his ships approached in the autumn of 1780, they were once again hit by a hurricane, and this time the fleet was virtually destroyed. In response, the British in Pensacola, under General John Campbell, launched an invasion of their own to attempt to recapture Mobile. Campbell sent some 500 British Regulars, Hessians, and Loyalist militia from Pennsylvania and Maryland, along with several hundred additional allied Choctaw warriors, under Captain Johann von Hanxleden to reclaim the town.

Hanxleden attacked on the morning of January 7, 1781. One group of Spanish tried to flee to the shore and were cut down, but the remaining troops inside the Fort (now renamed Fort Carlota) fought fiercely, killing 20 of the British attackers. Hanxleden decided the position was too strong to take, and withdrew back to Pensacola.

Later that spring, Galvez, reinforced by Spanish troops from Cuba, again sailed for Pensacola, and this time captured it after a short siege. At the end of the war, in 1783, Florida once again reverted back to Spanish rule.

Although the original Fort Charlotte is now long-gone (it was destroyed after being decommissioned by the US in 1823), an 80%-scale replica of it, reproducing about half of the structure, stands today at its old location in downtown Mobile. The reconstruction was built in 1976 as part of the city's Bicentennial celebrations. Two of the Fort's original French and British guns stand outside the rebuilt walls. Across the street, in Mardi Gras Park, is a small pile of collapsed brickwork—all that remains of the original Fort's walls.

Interpretive signs explain the history of the city's Revolutionary War battles and the various rooms and structures within the Fort. The site is now listed in the

National Register of Historic Places. To honor its historic past, the Fort is known for part of the year as Fort Conde and flies French flags, part of the year as Fort Charlotte and flies English flags, and part of the year as Fort Carlota and flies Spanish flags.

Cowpens

January 17, 1781

South Carolina

With the colonial win at Kings Mountain, the Revolutionary War in the south had reached a standoff. Rebel guerrillas owned the countryside, but were not strong enough to drive the British from their strongholds in the port cities. In December 1780, General Washington sent one of his best commanders, General Nathanael Greene, to South Carolina, hoping to break the stalemate. Upon arriving, Greene began to systematically consolidate all of the various irregular forces under his unified command, forming a new southern Continental Army.

In a bold strategic move, Greene then divided his tiny army. Around 1000 were sent with General Daniel Morgan, who had been captured at Quebec City during the failed invasion of Canada then exchanged in time to fight at Saratoga. Morgan was now based near Augusta, to forage for supplies, recruit new militiamen, and raise the spirits of local rebel supporters. Meanwhile, Greene would keep another force with him near Charleston. Cornwallis was therefore threatened from both sides: if he moved against Greene, Morgan's forces could seize Augusta: if he moved into the interior against Morgan, Greene could seize Charleston and cut him off from the coast.

Cornwallis, in desperation, divided his own forces. With 2000 troops, he stayed in Charleston, hoping to perhaps draw Greene into an open battle. At the same time, he sent one of his best units, the "British Legion" and some reinforcements, under Colonel Banastre Tarleton, to find Morgan's force. Known as "Bloody Ban" for his ruthless actions against colonial guerrillas and their supporters, Tarleton's men were a mix of British cavalry and Loyalist infantry recruited in Georgia and South Carolina.

The Cowpens battlefield

By the middle of January, Tarleton had caught up with Morgan's army. Knowing that Tarleton was nearby, Morgan formed his troops into a defensive line in a field pasture (known as a "cowpens") next to the Broad River in South Carolina.

Deciding that it would be better to make his stand here rather than risk being caught vulnerable while crossing the river, Morgan carefully arranged his troops. In the rear he put his Continental Army regulars; in front were the various local militia units. Knowing his man, Morgan correctly assumed that Tarleton would attack as soon as he arrived, charging aggressively straight into the colonial lines.

Right on cue, Tarleton marched all night to reach the battlefield and in the morning, seeing the Americans formed up in a line, launched his charge at the militia units, expecting them to panic and flee as they had at Camden.

Battlefield memorial

And then Morgan sprung his trap. Knowing that the militia were prone to break and run, he asked them to stand only long enough to fire two effective volleys and then retreat back through the American lines. As the militia began to fall back, the British, thinking that it was a rout, broke formation in pursuit and were drawn deeper and deeper into the American line, becoming more and more disorganized as they went. Morgan then sent both of his flanks on the attack.

At one point a group of soldiers, being ordered to turn and face a line of British, mistakenly interpreted it as a command to retreat and began to march away, pursued by the redcoats. But upon being ordered to halt and turn, they did, and fired a volley directly into the English. With fixed bayonets, the Continentals then fell upon the jumbled mass of British infantry and cavalry and surrounded them.

It became a slaughter. All of the British guns were captured. An American cavalry force rode around the rear of the British lines and cut off their retreat. Tarleton ordered the cavalry troopers from his Legion to attack, but instead they turned and fled. Tarleton himself was cut off and nearly captured before fighting his way out and escaping. In just half an hour, the British had lost an incredible 86% of their total force killed, wounded or captured. In essence, Tarleton's army no longer existed. Morgan had lost only 150 men.

Strategically, the Battle of Cowpens devastated the British. With the loss of Tarleton's forces, General Charles Cornwallis now no longer had sufficient troops to hold the Carolinas, and he decided to abandon Charleston and move his army into North Carolina to confront Greene's colonial forces there. It was the beginning of a chain of events that would end the Revolutionary War and win independence for the American colonies.

Today, the Cowpens National Battlefield Park is a National Historic Site. It was originally established by the War Department in 1929 and transferred to the National Park Service in 1933. The 850-acre park contains a Visitors Center and walking paths through the battleground. The 1860's Scruggs Cabin, which was not there at the time of the battle, is nevertheless reconstructed and preserved as a historic site.

Guilford Courthouse
March 15, 1781
North Carolina

Although the loss at Cowpens had crippled the British Army, General Charles Cornwallis was still determined to hold the strategic offensive, and decided to launch an expedition into North Carolina to confront the Continental Army there under General Nathanael Greene. Once he had joined up with General Daniel Morgan's forces, Greene embarked on a series of moves designed to lure Cornwallis further and further away from his supply bases in South Carolina. In February 1781, Cornwallis finally reached Greene's camp near Guilford Courthouse NC, but Greene retreated once more across the Dan River into Virginia, and Cornwallis, unable to follow, retreated to Hillsborough. Here he triumphantly declared that North Carolina was once again under English control, and issued a call for Loyalist militia. He got almost none.

Over the next few weeks, meanwhile, Greene was reinforced by militia units from Virginia and North

Carolina, and in mid-March he had a little over 2000 men, about as many as Cornwallis. After the colonials crossed back into North Carolina, further reinforcements swelled their force to 4000. Greene made his way back to Guilford Courthouse. Cornwallis, though outnumbered, moved to attack him there. The battle took place on March 15.

Guilford Courthouse stood at the intersection of two roads, with the American lines positioned along the crossroad. Greene's strategy was basically a re-play of that used by Morgan at Cowpens: the North Carolina militia were put in front, behind a fence, with orders to pull back during the fighting to lure the British into the rear line of Continental Army troops.

Memorials mark the position of the American militia

At one in the afternoon, Cornwallis opened the battle with a charge, expecting the militia to retreat. Instead, the

Americans fired several devastating musket volleys before falling back. The second line of militia, from Virginia, also fired and retreated. The British had hoped to make a bayonet charge, but the wooded areas of the battlefield were too dense for that. Redcoats began to falter and become disorganized as they were sucked deeper into the colonial lines. On the American left, the redcoats managed to capture some colonial cannons, but were then halted by the 1st Maryland Regiment. When Greene then launched a counter-assault with the rest of his Continentals, the English lines threatened to break.

The area of the initial British charge

Cornwallis saved himself with a desperate move: as the colonials began to push the British back, he ordered his cannons to fire directly into the struggling mass of soldiers. The hail of grapeshot killed English and American soldiers alike, but it did finally halt the colonial charge.

As Cornwallis struggled to reorganize his army, Greene decided that he had inflicted enough damage and, rather than risk another assault, he withdrew from the field. Cornwallis did not follow. The fighting had lasted about three hours, and the British had lost over 500 men, more than one-fourth of their total strength. It was a loss they could not afford. In his dispatches to London, Cornwallis claimed a victory, noting that his troops had pushed the Americans from the field. But as one MP declared in Parliament, the cost had been unacceptably high: "Another such victory would ruin the British Army."

After the battle, Cornwallis, located some 200 miles from his supply center, could not risk moving his battered force all the way back to Charleston, and now had no choice but to, in effect, abandon his base and retreat instead to the nearest seaport, at Wilmington NC. Greene and his army, meanwhile, rather than pursuing him there, continued to move down the coast towards Charleston and Savannah, hoping to draw Cornwallis into following him and exposing himself for another battle. But Cornwallis remained holed up in Wilmington and sent desperate messages to Clinton in New York for supplies and reinforcements.

Thus, although the Battle of Guilford Courthouse was a tactical defeat for the colonials, it was a major strategic win. Cornwallis's army was reduced to less than 2000 men and unable to move. Georgia and South Carolina were now held by only a small British garrison. Cornwallis's southern campaign was unraveling just as Burgoyne's New York campaign had, and all of the gains that the British had made since landing at Savannah had now been undone.

In 1887, a nonprofit citizens group called the Guilford Battle Ground Company was formed to protect and preserve the Guilford Courthouse site. The group managed to purchase 125 acres of historical land, and when the Guilford Courthouse National Military Park was established in 1917, the Company donated its purchases to the War Department.

Unfortunately, the commemorative markers and memorials which had been placed by the group were historically inaccurate and it was believed at that time that the battlefield area was much smaller than it actually was. As a result, encroaching development was allowed to consume some parts of the historical area, because it was not recognized as part of the site.

When the National Park Service took over in 1933, it made an effort to conduct research to determine the exact extent of the historical battlefield. Today, a new version of the Guilford Battlefield Company works with the NPS to raise money to purchase historically significant areas that are not yet part of the Park.

The Park contains a Visitors Center with exhibits, and a 2.5 mile loop trail that takes visitors to the major portions of the battlefield. Another part of the site is preserved by the nearby Greensboro County Park and the grounds of the Greensboro Science Center.

Eutaw Springs

September 8, 1781

South Carolina

When British General Charles Cornwallis had marched his army out of Charleston to engage General Nathanael Greene at Guilford Courthouse, he had left 8000 of his troops behind under General Francis Rawdon to protect his supply base. After Cornwallis retreated to the North Carolina coast following his defeat by Greene, then, Rawdon's force was the only thing standing between Greene and Savannah, and the colonials moved south, seeking to remove the British presence entirely from Georgia and South Carolina.

Though Rawdon's force outnumbered the colonials, it was scattered across several different locations, including Augusta and Fort Watson, and Greene spent several months systematically attacking and overrunning each of these outposts one at a time. (At Fort Watson, the colonials had built an old-fashioned siege tower, forcing the British to surrender without a shot.) By August 22, he had reached the old battle site at Camden.

Meanwhile, Rawdon had fallen sick and sailed home for England (he was captured by an American ship along the way), and command of the South Carolina forces fell to Lt Colonel Alexander Stewart. Stewart placed his remaining 2000 troops at Eutaw Springs, about 50 miles away from Charleston. Greene moved to attack him there.

Eutaw Springs Battlefield Park

At about 8 in the morning on September 8, a British foraging party ran into an American patrol, and the battle began. The British, under Maj. John Majoribanks, charged the American lines, but the militia units held their ground, and a counter-attack by the Continental Army regulars pushed the British back.

But when they reached the British campsite, the colonials, who had been on short supplies for some time, halted their assault to begin looting the tents for food and equipment. The British were able to regroup and occupy a nearby brick house, and from within its shelter they were able to pour fire onto the colonials. An American attempt to capture the house failed, and Greene withdrew his forces to another line a short distance away. He intended to attack again the next morning, but a weather front had moved in and, in the pouring rain, he withdrew instead, leaving the British in possession of the battlefield.

Grave of British Major Majoribanks

But once again, the British tactical victory had come at a crushing strategic cost. Stewart had lost 700 men out of 2000—one of the highest proportionate losses of the Revolutionary War. As his battered army limped back to Charleston, it was apparent that all of Georgia and South Carolina now belonged once again to the rebels. Greene had succeeded in driving the British out.

Most of the Eutaw Springs battleground has been lost. In 1970, the Eutaw Springs Battleground Park, consisting of four acres, was added to the National Register of Historic Places. It contains a number of memorials, some interpretive signs, and the grave of wounded British officer Maj. Majoribanks, who died shortly after the battle then was buried on a nearby plantation, and whose grave was relocated here after the area was flooded by a reservoir.

Today the Civil War Trust is actively raising money to purchase historically significant parcels to add to the park. When a steakhouse restaurant that was located inside the battlefield, near where the first clashes took place, closed and went out of business, the Trust was able to get a Federal matching grant and bought the property in 2017, with plans to tear down the restaurant, replant the area to its natural state, and incorporate it into the Battleground Park.

Yorktown

October 19, 1781

Virginia

Since the time of the fighting around Philadelphia and New Jersey in the summer of 1778, the Revolutionary War in the northern colonies had stalled. The British General Henry Clinton was holed up in New York—the only northern colonial city of any size that was still occupied by the English. Surrounding him was the Continental Army of General George Washington, based at West Point. In 1780 Washington had been joined by a contingent of 6000 French troops under Jean Baptiste de Rochambeau, who had landed at Rhode Island. The only other sizable British force remaining in the colonies was that of General Charles Cornwallis, holed up in Wilmington NC after his defeats at Cowpens and Guilford Courthouse.

In the winter of 1780, as part of its strategic focus on the southern colonies, the British Army had begun to move into Virginia. This was the largest and richest of the American colonies, and was supplying most of the men and funding for the Continental Congress. By holding Virginia, Clinton hoped he could cut off some of the support for the rebels, and also separate the northern colonies from the south. This would allow Cornwallis to land in Georgia, move through the Carolinas and hook up with him in Virginia, after which their combined army could move to Philadelphia and Boston, and then take on Washington and Rochambeau at New York.

In December 1780, a force of 1500 redcoats was landed at Portsmouth VA under the command of General Benedict Arnold—the former colonial hero of Saratoga who had turned to the British. Arnold began a series of raids in the surrounding countryside. A French fleet under Admiral Destouches was sent to carry 1200 troops under the Marquis de Lafayette to confront Arnold, but the British Navy turned back the French ships. Arnold was then reinforced in Virginia by another 2000 men, and General William Phillips took over command.

By this time, Cornwallis had been forced to retreat from Cowpens to Wilmington NC to keep his supply lines open, and now he had to make a strategic decision. Contrary to British hopes at the beginning of the southern campaign, the local people had not flocked to the Loyalist banner, and his remaining forces were no longer enough to hold the Carolinas. In any case, Cornwallis had concluded, it was impossible to defeat the colonials here unless their supply sources in Virginia were also removed.

And so, without orders from General Clinton, Cornwallis decided to abandon the Carolinas and move his troops into Virginia where they would join up with those of General Phillips. After a sea voyage and an overland march, Cornwallis arrived in Petersburg VA, near Richmond, and, after Arnold returned to New York and Phillips died of a fever, assumed command. He had a total of 8000 troops, including some 2000 Hessians.

His first move was against Lafayette, who was camped nearby with 3000 French and American troops. As Cornwallis approached, however, Lafayette decided to withdraw, pulling back and linking up with colonial garrisons commanded by Generals "Mad Anthony" Wayne and Friedrich Von Steuben. Cornwallis established a base nearby in Williamsburg VA.

French and American siege line

By this time, though, General Clinton was becoming worried by the French fleet in the Caribbean, which presented a threat to the British supply lines. In a series of orders, he sent Cornwallis to Yorktown, on the Chesapeake Bay, and dispatched engineers to begin constructing a port at which Royal Navy ships could deliver troops and protect the naval supply routes. It turned out to be a fatal move.

In New York, Generals Washington and Rochambeau had been planning a campaign to take New York City during the summer, but when word came that Cornwallis was immobilized in Yorktown, it presented a tempting target. The decision was sealed when the French Admiral Francois de Grasse agreed to move part of his fleet to Virginia, but only until October. (The Spanish, who had also entered the war against England, agreed to deploy their own fleet to protect the French possessions in the Caribbean, freeing up de Grasse's ships). The colonials and the French would, in a joint operation commanded by Washington, move their available forces to Yorktown.

Washington set out overland from New York on August 19 and reached Baltimore by mid-September. De Grasse's French fleet delivered reinforcements to Lafayette's army, then blockaded Chesapeake Bay to cut off Cornwallis's supply lines. In the most crucial action of the campaign, a British fleet under Admiral Thomas Graves attempted to break through the French blockade and re-establish contact with Cornwallis, but in the Battle of Chesapeake Bay on September 5, de Grasse defeated Graves and forced the British to sail back to New York. In this naval engagement, it could be argued, the French had won the American Revolutionary War. After the British fleet retreated, the French ships sailed to Chesapeake Bay to pick up Washington's Continental Army and Rochambeau's troops and bring them to Virginia. They arrived at Williamsburg on September 14 and marched to Yorktown by September 28.

Immediately, the combined French and American forces, totaling almost 20,000 men, began digging siege trenches. It was the first time since the disaster at Savannah that French and American combat forces operated directly together, but this time the work went smoothly. The French had extensive experience with

European-style sieges, and their engineers and sappers took charge of the operation.

Cornwallis had surrounded the town with a series of cannon redoubts, but now, outnumbered and surrounded, he realized that he did not have enough men to hold them all. Instead, he pulled back from his outer positions and concentrated his forces at his shorter inner line, anchored by Redoubt 9, Redoubt 10, and the Fusiliers Redoubt.

The French siege work was slow but steady. They dug a ring of protective trenches around Yorktown. By October 9, Washington's artillery was in range and began bombarding Yorktown. Meanwhile, the engineers inched forward through "zigzag" ditches, thus working their way ever closer and closer, and work was begun on another line of siege trenches, just out of British musket range. Once it was finished, Cornwallis realized, the colonials and their French supporters would move up their cannons and blow his defenses to pieces.

Reconstructed Redoubt 10

On October 14, the British Redoubts 9 and 10, the only remaining obstacles to the second siege line, were captured in a night attack by French and American troops. In desperation, Cornwallis first tried to launch an assault to capture the siege guns that were pounding his position, and, when that failed, tried to break through the line of French and American troops and open a pathway for a retreat across the York River. With these defeats, all hope ended, and Cornwallis knew it was all over. On October 17, a British drummer approached the American trenches with a white flag.

The following day, representatives from the British, American and French armies met at the nearby Moore House and worked out the terms. At the formal surrender ceremony the next day, Cornwallis pleaded that he was too sick to attend, and sent his second-in-command instead. Still refusing to acknowledge the American independence, British General Charles O'Hara tried to present Cornwallis's sword to the French General Rochambeau: Rochambeau in turn refused to accept it, and pointed to General Washington. But Washington, miffed by Cornwallis's absence, also refused to accept it, and turned to his own second-in-command, General Benjamin Lincoln. According to legend, which is probably apocryphal, as the British troops marched out of Yorktown to stack their muskets in surrender, the regimental band played a popular tune of the day, "The World's Turned Upside Down".

In 1930, the Yorktown battlefield was incorporated into the Colonial History National Monument under management of the National Park Service (which also includes the Jamestown settlement). The Yorktown Cemetery was transferred from the Defense Department to the NPS three years later, and in 1936 the expanded Monument became a National Historical Park. There is a

Visitors Center and a seven-mile driving tour that covers the battlefield, including the Nelson House where Cornwallis stayed during the battle, and the Moore House where the surrender negotiations took place. The siege trenches and earthworks were restored in 1976.

The American in the Tower of London

1781

London

There are not many Revolutionary War sites in London, but one of them is the most famous landmark in the city. In its long history, the Tower of London became notorious as a jail for English traitors and as a site for executions, but the celebrated prison only ever held one American.

In 1779, France and Spain were already involved with the war against England, and were sending money and weapons to the American rebels. Realizing that the Netherlands also had grievances against the British, the colonial government in Philadelphia opened secret talks with the Dutch government, hoping to bring them into the conflict as well. In the fall of 1779, Henry Laurens, a wealthy South Carolinian slave trader who had served as President of the Continental Congress, was dispatched to Amsterdam to begin negotiations towards an alliance.

The talks were successful, and in August 1780 Laurens set sail back to America with a draft treaty that would bring military and economic aid from the Dutch, including a large loan and a commercial trade agreement. But Laurens' ship, the *Mercury*, was intercepted off the coast of Newfoundland on September 3 by the British Navy frigate *Vestal*. As Royal Marines boarded the ship, Laurens tried to throw the secret diplomatic papers overboard to prevent their capture, but the English sailors were able to recover them. The news of a pending Dutch-American alliance surprised the British, and in response the Crown Government declared war on the Netherlands, the fourth of what had become a series of Anglo-Dutch Wars.

Tower of London

Although Laurens considered himself to be a legitimate diplomat and entitled to immunity, the British treated him as a mere rebellious traitor, and arrested him. Laurens was taken to England and held at Scotland Yard for a short time, then was formally charged with treason—a capital offense—and transferred to the Tower of London.

The Continental Congress protested both Laurens' arrest and the conditions under which he was being kept. Locked away in one of the stone turrets, he was deprived of writing materials and also denied mail. He later recorded that the marching band of redcoat soldiers who stood guard in the Tower courtyard often played "Yankee Doodle" to mock him. Laurens was allowed to have visitors, however, and one of these, a wealthy English merchant named Richard Oswald who had previously been his business partner, tried to argue on his behalf to members of Parliament. Laurens became such a celebrity that he was able to pose for a painted portrait while in prison.

On December 31, 1781, after being held in the Tower for fifteen months, an agreement was finally worked out in which Laurens was released in exchange for the surrendered British General Lord Charles Cornwallis, who was being held by the Americans. After being freed, Laurens sailed to Amsterdam to raise money for the colonial rebels, then returned to Philadelphia. In 1783 he sailed back to Europe as part of the American delegation at the peace talks in Paris. Due to delays, however, he arrived just two days before the final draft treaty was settled.

Cape Canaveral

March 10, 1783

Florida

The last battle of the American Revolutionary War was a naval engagement off the coast of Florida—which took place a month after the war had officially ended.

After the surrender of General Charles Cornwallis at Yorktown in 1781, the only remaining British force in the colonies was that of General Henry Clinton in New York City. Clinton was in turn already surrounded by American and French forces under General Washington, who was making plans to attack in the spring of 1782. But when word reached New York that peace negotiations had begun in Paris, Washington suspended his plans. Although France and Spain, who were both at war with England, continued military operations elsewhere in the world, in North America things came to a standstill.

After a time, Washington, recognizing that the British forces in New York were incapable of action, concluded that the Continental Army was now unnecessary and asked the Continental Congress to disband it and release his troops from service. Many in Congress, however, felt that the Paris negotiations would probably fail, and they decided to keep the Army intact just in case hostilities started up again.

But there was an awkward problem. The Continental Congress had no authority to levy taxes, and had been financing the war largely through loans from France and Spain. But as the fighting shifted elsewhere, this money dried up, and the Americans found themselves nearly broke. And so, as the Continental Regulars remained camped around New York for month after month, the Congress had no money with which to pay them. And as the negotiations in Paris dragged out, the troops, who had now been without pay for almost two years, began to get restless. There had already been a series of mutinies in the Army: at one point a unit of militia had marched partway to Philadelphia, determined to force Congress to pay them.

The problem was finally solved by Robert Morris, an American shipping mogul and financier who had extensive connections to ports around the world. By January 1783, Morris had worked out a deal with Spain for a loan of $72,000 to be used to pay the Continental troops. He separately dispatched two ships, the USS *Alliance* under Captain John Barry and the USS *Duc de Lauzun* under Captain John Green, to pick up the money in Havana. The *Duc de Lauzun* arrived there first and was loaded with crates of Spanish silver coins. She left Cuba on March 6, escorted by the *Alliance*, and sailed for Philadelphia.

But the British had received intelligence about the mission, and the next day the two American ships were approached by the 32-gun frigate HMS *Alarm* and the 28-gun frigate HMS *Sybil*, under Captain James Vashon. The

Americans turned back towards Cuba and the protection of the French and Spanish fleets there, and the British did not pursue them.

The next day, the Americans tried again. This time, to lighten the ponderously-slow *Duc de Lauzun*, the silver coins were transferred to the *Alliance*, and most of the *Lauzun's* cannons were thrown overboard. Both ships then proceeded up the Florida coast.

Commemorative plaque at Cape Canaveral marking the battle

On March 10, they encountered the British again, about 100 miles off Cape Canaveral. The *Alarm* and *Sybil* had now been joined by the 18-gun sloop *Tobago*. But as the English fleet moved in, another ship appeared in the distance. The Americans were unable to make out who it was, but the British commander Vashon could see that it was a French warship, the *Triton*. This caused the *Alarm* and *Tobago* to hold back, and Captain Barry, on the USS

Alliance, saw his chance. Maneuvering his ship between the *Duc de Lauzun* and the British *Sybil*, he made a dash through the English fleet. After a 40-minute firefight, the *Sybil* withdrew, and the two American ships, now joined by the *Triton*, made their way on to Philadelphia.

It wasn't until after they reached port that they heard that the Treaty of Paris, ending the war, had already been signed on February 3.

Today, a memorial plaque in Titusville FL, on Cape Canaveral, commemorates the last battle of the Revolutionary War.

Treaty of Paris

Cornwallis's surrender in October 1781, along with Clinton's effective encirclement in New York City, essentially ended the British military presence in the North American colonies, and the Revolutionary War was all but over. But it was almost two years before peace was finally concluded.

Part of the reason was military: although the fighting in North America had ended, the war of which it had become only one theater continued, and the French and Spanish maintained military operations against England in Africa, Asia and Europe. In particular, Spain was conducting a long siege against Gibraltar, and did not want to end the war until she had captured that strategic island from the British. In the end, however, the siege, though it continued right up to the end of the war, failed.

Formal peace negotiations began in Paris in April 1782, with representatives from Britain on one side and those from France, the United States, Spain and the Netherlands (all of whom were at war with England) on the other. France took the lead in representing the warring nations, and made the initial peace proposal on behalf of the colonies. The United States was to be recognized as an independent country. The area west of the Appalachian Mountains would be established as a homeland for all of the various Native American tribes east of the Mississippi (many of whom had fought on the side of the English), with the northern half of this Indian Nation under the protection of England and the southern half under a Spanish protectorate.

This proposal, however, was opposed by France's own allies, especially the United States, and the negotiations broke down as each ally, suspicious of French motives, asserted its own interests. Eventually the joint negotiations ended, and each country began working out its own independent peace terms. The process took over a year.

The United States delegation, headed by Benjamin Franklin, opened its negotiations in September 1782 by demanding not only independence, but also large territorial concessions from England. All of Canada was to become a US province, and the US was to also gain ownership of the land it controlled from the Ohio River Valley and the Great Lakes down to Kentucky. For Britain, the sticking points centered around the rights of Loyalists and those Americans who had been opposed to independence. Many of these had been arrested and their property confiscated by the colonial governments, and England now demanded a general amnesty and the return of their seized assets.

After much compromising on both sides, a preliminary agreement was reached. England would recognize American independence. Canada would remain under British rule, but the US would retain fishing rights in Canadian territorial waters. All of the land south of Canada, north of Florida and east of the

Mississippi would become US territory, all of the existing British forts and trade outposts there would be removed, and the US would have the right to access the Mississippi River at New Orleans. The US Congress would "sincerely recommend" to the state governments that they return the confiscated property of the Loyalists and grant them amnesty as American citizens. And all British Army property in the colonies (including the slaves that had joined with it) was to remain and be turned over to the US.

In separate treaties, the English Crown then agreed to peace terms with the other combatants. The African territories of Senegal and Tobago were turned over to the French, and several other territories in Africa and the Caribbean were exchanged between the two countries. The British territory in Florida and the island of Minorca was turned over to Spain. The islands of Grenada and the Bahamas would be returned to British control, and all the European powers agreed to recognize British authority over all of India. The parts of the Dutch East Indies that had been seized by the English would be returned to the Netherlands.

The formal Treaty of Paris went into effect upon being ratified by all the parties on February 3, 1783. The Revolutionary War was over, and a new nation—the United States of America—was born.

Much of the Treaty, however, was destined to be broken by both parties. The United States refused to offer a general amnesty to the Loyalists or to return their confiscated property, and over 100,000 of them left for Canada. The British did not remove their forts in the Ohio River Valley, and, still holding on to their desire for an independent Indian Nation, eventually began to ally itself with the various Native American tribes both in that area and in the Southeast who were resisting American encroachment. England also refused to hand over any of the thousands of African-American slaves who had been granted their freedom by joining with the British: these freed slaves were instead moved to Canada, Europe, or the Caribbean. The United States, meanwhile, never gave up its hopes to obtain Canada, and continued to maintain a string of military forts along the northern border.

By 1812, all of these tensions would eventually lead to another war between the United States of America and Great Britain.

www.ingramcontent.com/pod-product-compliance
Lightning Source LLC
LaVergne TN
LVHW051546070426
835507LV00021B/2432